101 KEY IDEAS

Economics

101 KEY IDEAS

Economics

Keith Brunskill

LEARNING RESOURCES
CENTRE
Havering College
of Further and Higher Education

TEACH YOURSELF BOOKS

330

AG

28395

Acknowledgements

I would like to thank the publishers for the opportunity to write this book and Jane, Dave and Paul for their encouragement. Thanks to all my former students who played a part in my rethinking of the content and presentation of economics, so that studying it can be an enjoyable experience. Any errors in the text prove that we are always learning. My hope is that this introduction will help you understand some key ideas and encourage further study,

For UK order queries: please contact Bookpoint Ltd, 130 Milton Park, Abingdon, Oxon OX14 4SB. Telephone: (44) 01235 827720. Fax: (44) 01235 400454. Lines are open from 9.00–18.00, Monday to Saturday, with a 24-hour message answering service. Email address: orders@bookpoint.co.uk

For USA order queries: please contact McGraw-Hill Customer Services, P.O. Box 545, Blacklick, OH 43004-0545, USA. Telephone: 1-800-722-4726. Fax: 1-614-755-5645.

For Canada order queries: please contact McGraw-Hill Ryerson Ltd., 300 Water St, Whitby, Ontario L1N 9B6, Canada. Telephone: 905 430 5000. Fax: 905 430 5020.

Long-renowned as the authoritative source for self-guided learning – with more than 30 million copies sold worldwide – the *Teach Yourself* series includes over 300 titles in the fields of languages, crafts, hobbies, business and education.

British Library Cataloguing in Publication Data
A catalogue entry for this title is available from The British Library.

Library of Congress Catalog Card Number: on file

First published in UK 2001 by Hodder Headline Plc, 338 Euston Road, London NW1 3BH.

First published in US 2001 by Contemporary Books, a division of the McGraw-Hill Companies, 4255 West Touhy Avenue, Lincolnwood (Chicago), Illinois 60712–1975, USA.

The 'Teach Yourself' name and logo are registered trade marks of Hodder & Stoughton Ltd.

Copyright © 2001 Keith Brunskill

In UK: All rights reserved. No part of this publication may be reproduced or transmitted in any form or by any means, electronic or mechanical, including photocopy, recording, or any information storage and retrieval system, without permission in writing from the publisher or under licence from the Copyright Licensing Agency Limited. Further details of such licences (for reprographic reproduction) may be obtained from the Copyright Licensing Agency Limited of 90 Tottenham Court Road, London W1P 9HE.

In US: All rights reserved. Except as permitted under the United States Copyright Act of 1976, no part of this publication may be reproduced or distributed in any form or by any means, or stored in a database or retrieval system, without the prior written permission of Contemporary Books.

Cover design and illustration by Mike Stones
Typeset by Transet Limited, Coventry, England.
Printed in Great Britain by Cox & Wyman Ltd, Reading, Berkshire.

Impression number   10 9 8 7 6 5 4 3 2 1
Year   2006   2005   2004   2003   2002   2001

Contents

Adam Smith's Economics   1

Ageing Population   2

Aggregate Demand   3

Aggregate Supply   4

Balance of Payments   5

Barriers to Entry   6

Budgets and Mini Budgets   7

Business Cycle and Recession   8

Central Bank   9

Circular Flow of Income   10

Classical and New Classical
   Economics 11

Collusion and Cartels   12

Common Argricultural Policy   13

Comparative Advantage   14

Competition Policy and
   Contestable Markets   15

Consumer Expenditure   16

Cost Benefit Analysis   17

Cost Push Inflation   18

Costs of Production   19

Crowding Out Theory   20

Deindustrualization   21

Demand Pull Inflation   22

Demerit Goods   23

Development Economics   24

Direct Taxation   25

Econimic Activity Rates   26

Economic Growth   27

Economic Systems   28

Economies of Scale   29

Efficiency   30

Elasticity   31

Entrepreneurship   32

Environmental Economics   33

Equilibrium   34

EU and the EURO   35

Exchange Rates   36

Externalities   37

Factors of Production   38

Firms' Objectives   39

Firms' Revenue   40

Fiscal Policy   41

Free Trade and Protectionism   42

Full Employment and Types of
   Unemployment   43

Globalization   44

Government Borrowing and the
   National Debt   45

Government Expenditure   46

Gross National Product   47

Health Economics   48

Horizontal, Vertical and Lateral
   Integration   49

Income and Wealth   50
Indirect Taxation   51
Inflation: Meaning and
    Measurement   52
Injections and Leakages   53
Innovation   54
Interest Rates   55
International Competitiveness   56
Investment   57
Keynesian Economics   58
Labour Mobility   59
Macroeconomics   60
Marginal Analysis   61
Market Demand   62
Market Failure and Government
    Intervention   63
Market Mechanism   64
Market Supply   65
Merit Goods   66
Microeconomics   67
Minimum Wage   68
Monetarism and Monetary Policy
    69
Monopolistic Competition   70
Monopoly   71
Multinationals   72
Multiplier Effect   73
North South Divide and Regional
    Policy   74

Oil Crisis   75
Oligopoly   76
Opportunity Cost   77
Perfect Competition   78
Philips Curve   79
Policy Conflicts   80
Poverty   81
Price Discrimination   82
Privatization and Deregulation   83
Profits and Profit Maximization
84
Public Goods   85
Real and Money Values   86
Savings   87
Scarcity   88
Stakeholding Economy   89
Standard of Living   90
Stocks and Shares   91
Supply Side Policies   92
Sustainability   93
Third World Debt   94
Trade Unions   95
Transfer Payments and Income
    Redistribution   96
Transition Economics   97
Transport Economics   98
Urban Policy   99
Wage Differentials   100
Welfare State   101

Introduction

Welcome to the **Teach Yourself 101 Key Ideas** series. We hope that you will find both this book and others in the series to be useful, interesting and informative. The purpose of the series is to provide an introduction to a wide range of subjects, in a way that is entertaining and easy to absorb.

Each book contains 101 short accounts of key ideas or terms which are regarded as central to that subject. The accounts are presented in alphabetical order for ease of reference. All of the books in the series are written in order to be meaningful whether or not you have previous knowledge of the subject. They will be useful to you whether you are a general reader, are on a pre-university course, or have just started at university.

We have designed the series to be a combination of a text book and a dictionary. We felt that many text books are too long for easy reference, while the entries in dictionaries are often too short to provide sufficient detail. The **Teach Yourself 101 Key Ideas** series gives the best of both worlds! Here are books that you do not have to read cover to cover, or in any set order. Dip into them when you need to know the meaning of a term, and you will find a short, but comprehensive account which will be of real help with those essays and assignments. The terms are described in a straightforward way with a careful selection of academic words thrown in for good measure!

So if you need a quick and inexpensive introduction to a subject, **Teach Yourself 101 Key Ideas** is for you. And incidentally, if you have any suggestions about this book or the series, do let us know. It would be great to hear from you.

Best wishes with your studies!

Paul Oliver
Series Editor

Adam Smith's Economics

Over his lifetime, Adam Smith's economic investigations ranged from the theory of trade, to economic growth and an attempt to model the workings of the economy. His contribution to economic thought stemmed from a central belief that a *free market*, or capitalist economic system, would maximize the welfare of the population. In 1776 he published the *Inquiry into the Nature and Causes of the Wealth of Nations*. In it he argued that people taking part in market exchange always act selfishly but that the outcome is in everyone's interest because the resulting economic growth raises living standards. It followed from this idea that the role of government in the economy should be minimal, confined to the provision of defence, justice, and public works such as roads and bridges. The only market intervention should be to prevent monopoly and to promote competition, which would increase business efficiency.

His major insight into the production system was the principle of the division of labour.

By splitting production up and getting workers to specialize on a single task, factory owners would see a rise in workers' productivity. This combined with technical progress was a key to economic growth. He recognized that the size of markets was a constraint on growth and therefore developed the idea that free trade between nations was central to economic progress.

In the field of public finance, Smith was interested in how the tax system should operate. The basic rules or canons of taxation that he published were an attempt to make the tax system both fair and efficient.

Adam Smith was perhaps the founding father of economics as an academic discipline. It is a tribute to the strength of his ideas that they continue to influence economic policy.

see also...

Market Mechanism; Economic Growth; Competition Policy and Contestable Markets

Ageing Population

The size of a country's population can be a source of economic strength or weakness, depending on the availability of other resources. Any change in size will be accompanied by a change in the age distribution. The age structure of a population can be illustrated by a population pyramid, which is a bar chart showing the number of people in each age group. It is divided into males and females because the ratio of males to females is different according to age. The shape of the pyramid depends on the relationship between the birth and death rates. Under conditions of high birth and high death rates it will have a classic pyramid shape. In rich advanced western economies the trend has been for the birth rate to fall which narrows the base of the pyramid. At the same time, the fall in the death rate as life expectancy rises leads to the pyramid bulging at the top end, with women on average living longer than men.

The ageing population has become an economic issue because of its impact on the health service and the social security system. If the proportion of people of non-working age rises, relative to the 16–65 age group, it can put economic pressure on the working population to increase its productivity. The extra resources necessary to support the elderly may lead to higher taxation on the working population, or the government may have to alter the composition of its spending, reducing some programmes to fund the expansion of others. It may be a good idea to increase the size of the working population by raising the retirement age. The size of the working population can be increased by raising the economic activity rate of women. Recently there has been discussion of a pensions crisis caused by the ageing population. In future, people may have to supplement the basic state retirement pension from savings or private pension plans.

see also...

Economic Activity Rates; Transfer Payments and Income Redistribution; Welfare State

Aggregate Demand

Agregate demand is the total flow of money expenditure on domestically produced goods and services in the economy at any particular time. It determines the actual level of income in the economy and plays a major part in determining the current level of employment. The biggest component of aggregate demand is the flow of consumer expenditure (C). In addition, there is the amount spent by the business sector on investment (I). The government expenditure (G) represents the flow of spending on goods and services. The money it spends on benefits or transfer payments will be reflected in the amount of consumer expenditure. In an economy with foreign trade, the expenditure flow is influenced by exports (X) and imports (M). It is the difference between these two, or the net exports, that is added to the other components of aggregate demand.

$$AD = C + I + G + X - M.$$

Fluctuations in any of its components will influence the state of the trade or business cycle. The level of economic activity can move in a boom and bust fashion if aggregate demand is not carefully managed.

In general, an economy will perform efficiently when the level of aggregate demand exactly matches the aggregate supply or the potential output of the economic resources. If the actual output resulting from aggregate expenditure is less than the potential output, then there is a recessionary or deflationary gap. The government can devise policies to influence each component, or a combination of them, in order to get closer to a full employment of resources. The opposite action must be taken to reduce the flow of spending if aggregate demand rises faster than the productive capacity. Fiscal and monetary measures will try to prevent the economy overheating and experiencing demand pull inflation.

see also...

Fiscal Policy; Monetarism and Monetary Policy; Aggregate Supply

Aggregate Supply

Aggregate supply represents the total productive capacity of an economy, based on its present resources or factors of production, i.e. land, labour, capital and enterprise. Aggregate supply will increase if the quantity of resources rises, or as a result of higher productivity from a given volume of resources. The level of capital investment, together with the growth in technical knowledge, will be the main influence on the growth of aggregate supply. An economy will be in macroeconomic equilibrium where the level of aggregate demand or total expenditure matches the aggregate supply or the potential output. It is the resulting level of GDP that effectively determines the ruling price level in the economy.

Changes in aggregate supply can be caused by *supply shocks*. Short-term economic events such as an oil crisis or a sudden surge in wage demands, can cause production costs in the economy to rise. There may be a significant fall in output as a consequence, putting upward pressure on the price level.

There can be positive supply shocks. A sudden investment boom resulting from a fall in interest rates, could trigger a rise in aggregate supply and reduce the inflation rate. If the aggregate supply is rising over time, the economy will be experiencing economic growth. Since the 1980s, there has been an increase in interest in what have been labelled *supply side policies* as a better way of managing the economy rather than manipulating the level of aggregate demand. Demand and supply side measures are best seen as complementary rather than as substitutes in managing the economy so that the broad objectives of government economic policy can be achieved simultaneously.

see also...

Supply Side Policies; Aggregate Demand; Economic Growth

Balance of Payments

This is the summary of all the external transactions of the residents of an economy in the course of one year. Any money leaving the country is a *debit* item in the accounts, whilst inflows are a *credit*. The government's objective is to get a balance of payments equilibrium, meaning that the money flowing in to the economy should equal the outflows. Persistent surplus or deficit can cause economic problems and can damage the other objectives. In Britain, as the value of imports exceeds that of exports there is a deficit on the balance of trade and hence a deficit in the balance of payments accounts. There are also income flows in the form of wages, interest and profits flowing in and out of the economy and international transfers of money. The sum of all the trade and money flows is the *current account* of the balance of payments.

The *capital account* records money flows from buying and selling assets, the transfer of money by migrants, overseas aid, and dealings with the EU. The third part of the accounts records the flow of direct investment in business capital and the flow of money going into shares, bonds and bank deposits. The last item is sometimes called hot money, indicating how quickly it can move location if relative interest rates and exchange rates alter.

An overall deficit on the balance of payments can be financed by running down the official reserves of foreign currencies, borrowing from abroad or taking action to stop the root cause. The main weapons a government has to influence imports and exports are monetary and fiscal measures and perhaps the ability to alter the exchange rate. The inflow of financial investment can be increased by raising the interest rate. The overall balance of payments must balance. The problem lies in the costs of getting the total credits to equal the total debits.

see also...

Exchange Rates; Free Trade and Protectionism

Barriers to Entry

Barriers are a mixture of obstacles that deter or prevent new firms from entering a market to compete with the existing firms. A firm may be protected by legal barriers such as a government license to produce or the existence of a patent on its product or production methods. High fixed cost or setup cost in activities, such as electricity generation, aircraft and car production, may deter potential entrants. Only very large firms will be able to fund the necessary investment. Research and development cost will represent a high proportion of total cost and it is the risk of losing this investment that deters new entrants. Brand names with a high degree of consumer loyalty reinforced by advertising may prove a difficult obstacle to overcome. This explains why firms regard their expenditure on advertising and promotions as an act of investment. Existing firms can make entry more difficult through brand proliferation, giving the customers an apparent abundance of choice and closing market niches. Economies of scale can be a barrier because the existing large producers are able to produce at a lower average cost than those firms just starting up.

Some existing firms may have a monopoly access to raw materials, components or retail outlets, making it difficult for new entrants to compete. Vertically integrated manufacturing businesses will be protected by the fact that their rivals' costs will be higher.

Where barriers to entry are high, the market structure will be clear to that of oligopoly where a few large firms dominate the market. New entrants will only appear, if they expect the economic returns to be greater than the cost of breaking the entry barriers.

see also...

Economies of Scale; Costs of Production; Monopoly

Budgets and Mini Budgets

The budget is an occasion when the Chancellor of the Exchequer delivers a short summary of current economic performance and forecasts for the next year. This is to give a context for the expenditure and taxation plans. The principal task is to show how the government expenditure will be financed. If the two flows of money do not match, there will either be a *budget deficit* or a *budget surplus*. A budget deficit is where spending exceeds tax revenue and the difference will have to be borrowed. A budget surplus would give the government an opportunity to pay back some debt. The current thinking is that budget deficits should be avoided in order to reduce borrowing as a proportion of GDP.

The Labour government's policy is that over the course of the trade cycle, it will only borrow money for capital investment, not to finance current expenditure. The budget is an annual event, but, in the past, governments have reacted to changing economic conditions by having mini budgets to fine tune the economy. Fine tuning is now done mainly by changing the rate of interest rather than by altering taxes and spending.

Some of the government's spending and taxation can act as automatic stabilizers on the level of economic activity reducing the need for frequent tax changes. Unemployment benefit spending rises automatically when the economy is in recession. At the same time revenues from taxation will fall. Both effects slow the rate at which income falls. In a boom, the opposite happens and the expansion is automatically slowed down. The budget can be a vehicle for the introduction of new taxes to widen the tax base. The pattern of taxation ie the balance between direct taxes on income and indirect taxes on goods and services can also be changed.

see also...

Fiscal Policy; Government Expenditure; Direct Taxation; Indirect Taxation

Business Cycle and Recession

The terms business cycle or trade cycle, are labels to describe the fluctuations in GDP that have occurred in the economy since records began. There have been many theories offered to explain them, and many attempts by governments to modify them. The economic instability must be due to shock factors affecting the aggregate demand or the aggregate supply in the economy. A recession is where there is a fall in GDP over three successive quarters of a year. Changes in any of the expenditure flows will cause a new equilibrium income where actual output does not match potential output.

Recessions can be triggered by events in international trade, such as a sudden fall in exports. World recessions occur because of events affecting all economies, or because domestic recessions in major economies can get socially transmitted through the trade process. In this case, it is not easy for national governments acting alone to stimulate an economic recovery. The downturns in economic activity vary in their depth and the time they last. The British economy experienced recessions in the early years of the 1980s and 1990s. Government can help speed up the economic recovery by using discretionary fiscal policy in the form of tax reductions or increases in its expenditure. A reduction in interest rates may also have an expansionary impact. Once underway, a recovery gathers pace because of a multiplier effect. Any increases in government spending, investment or exports will lead to a greater than proportional rise in national income. Economists have found it difficult to explain the exact turning points in the business cycle. The answer may lie in psychology rather than economics, with people taking action, that brings about either what they hoped for in an upturn or what they feared in a downturn. Governments trying to stabilise the business cycle, must ensure that their policy does not damage their other economic objectives.

see also...

Multiplier Effect; Fiscal Policy; Gross National Product

Central Bank

The Bank of England is the central bank of the British economy and it fulfils several economic functions. It is banker to both central government and the commercial banks. Its main responsibility is for the conduct of monetary policy. Since 1997, the central bank has been independent of the government. It is expected to pursue a strict anti-inflation monetary policy, keeping the annual rate of price rises below 2.5%, a target set by the government. The chosen instrument is changes in interest rates or the current price of money. The idea behind central bank independence is a belief that elected governments have an incentive to run monetary policy with a bias towards inflation when pursuing economic and social objectives. It is also in line with possible entry into the EMU where an unelected central bank operates monetary policy.

The Bank of England still retains control over the issue of banknotes and will act as lender of last resort to the banking system in the case of a major bank collapse. It holds the commercial banks' operational balances. These deposits are used in a clearing system to settle inter-bank debt on a daily basis. Managing the national debt is now done by the Debt Management Office, an arm of the Treasury. The Financial Services Authority now has responsibility for supervising the conduct of financial institutions. The idea is that the central bank should have no conflicts of interest and be able to focus entirely on its main objective. In the past, when the government has been operating a managed exchange rate, the Bank of England has intervened as its agent in the foreign exchange market to influence the external value of the currency. Every economy has to have some form of central bank performing similar tasks to ensure the smooth running of the whole financial system.

see also...

Aggregate Demand; Interest Rates; Exchange Rates

Circular Flow of Income

Aggregate expenditure in the economy is made of C+I+G+X−M. Changes in national income can be seen as the result of interaction between the injections into the circular flow I+G+X

and the leakages from it, i.e. S+M+T.

Equilbrium income is therefore where I+G+X = S+M+T.

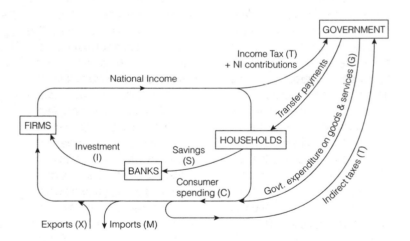

see also...

Aggregate Demand; Injections and Leakages

Classical and New Classical Economics

Classical economists studied the relationship between population, the accumulation of capital, technology and economic growth. One of the key theories was the law of comparative advantage that justified the principle of specialization and free trade. There was a fundamental belief in the efficiency of free markets, and classical economists saw only a minimal role for government. Says Law suggested that macroeconomic equilibrium was guaranteed because supply creates its own demand. The production system, in making the output, also generated the income with which the goods and services could be purchased. Classical economic analysis assumed that prices and wages were flexible and that changes in the conditions of demand and supply would always return the economy to its original equilibrium. It was only fluctuations in the trade cycle that would create temporary unemployment. It was Keynesian economics which provided the main challenge to this view of how the economy operated. It is in the discussion of inflation and unemployment that part of classical thought has continued to the present time.

The new classical school believes that if the economy has unemployment higher than the natural rate, this must be voluntary unemployment and workers could be priced back into work by accepting a cut in real wages. The new classical macroeconomic view is that government policy should control inflation through tight monetary policy and boost the aggregate supply through supply side policies. Expansionary fiscal policy may simply trigger demand pull inflation. A better option is to reduce the natural rate of unemployment by making labour markets operate more efficiently.

see also...

Inflation: Meaning and Measurement; Full Employment and Types of Unemployment

Collusion and Cartels

When particular industries are dominated by a handful of firms, the situation is one of *oligopoly*. The most important feature of the market structure is that these firms are interdependent. Each firm's competitive strategy is influenced by the anticipated action of the others. It is the uncertainty of outcome which makes competitive behaviour risky. This gives close rivals an incentive to limit the form and degree of competition, i.e. to collude in some way. This is different from cooperation, because it implies an attempt to make the market operate to benefit producers at the expense of consumers. Collusion is therefore an anti-competitive practice which may be illegal. This is why real world collusion is tacit or informal, with no written agreement.

Collusion may be the result of a price war that has reduced profits to a point where it is in all the firms' interests to make an agreement over the price they charge. Price leadership is a form of collusive behaviour. It is difficult to prove the existence of price agreements because similar prices can either be the result of a highly competitive market or collusion. Simultaneous price changes are not always evidence of collusion because there may be cost changes that have affected all firms in the market, e.g. petrol retailers are bound to alter their prices in line with changes in the world price of oil.

A cartel is a formal association of producers which exists to manage the total output or the price of the product. The most famous example is OPEC (Organisation of Petroleum Exporting Countries) which agrees production quotas for members using the economic logic that a reduction in supply will force up the market price. Cartels are an attempt to increase market power, there is always an incentive for individual members to cheat on the agreement, by undercutting an agreed price, or exceeding the quota to increase revenue.

see also...

Oligopoly

Common Agricultural Policy

The original idea behind the CAP was to protect farmers' incomes within the EU and therefore guarantee a secure supply of food. The EU is not alone in protecting its agriculture, but it is the extent and the form of protection which has been criticized. Not all regions of the EU have the same degree of efficiency in agriculture and in some areas the activity accounts for a large percentage of total employment.

The basic economic problem is that the world price of foodstuffs is lower than the EU price. The EU market is protected by import tariffs and the export of food from the EU is subsidized. This in itself is a cause of economic tension in world trade. Economic theory suggests that an artificial price above the market equilibrium will encourage supply and discourage demand. The excess production has taken the form of food mountains and wine lakes. These surpluses were either stored, destroyed or dumped at subsidized prices on the world market. One way of removing the excess supply is to reduce the area of land that is cultivated. This supply-side solution has been achieved through set-aside schemes and the imposition of production quotas. The alternative policy of stimulating the demand for food is less likely to work. A further reform has been to gradually negotiate lower guaranteed prices. The latest policy is to replace price guarantees with direct income payments to the poorer farmers and to increase regional aid to rural areas. One of the obstacles to reform is the prospect of EU enlargement. This is bound to increase the supply of foodstuffs and some of the new entrants may be higher cost producers. The CAP accounts for over half the EU budget, and its operating cost is bound to rise. There may be disagreement over how it will be financed and the prospect of getting agreement over reform may diminish as the membership increases.

see also...

EU and the EURO

Comparative Advantage

This idea dates from the early nineteenth century with the theories of David Ricardo, extending Adam Smith's work on the principle of *specialization*. The theory of comparative advantage attempted to explain why countries specialized and engaged in *free trade* and how they chose what to specialize in. The idea was that two countries might be able to produce the same products using the same number of resources. If one could produce more than the other this was an absolute advantage and reflected greater efficiency. The principle of comparative advantage suggested that even if this occurred it would still pay both countries to specialize in what they did best for export, and to import the other product.

The explanation lay in the relative efficiency with which one good was produced, compared with the other. If the domestic opportunity cost of making a product differed from one country to another, then there was an opportunity for specialization and the trade could benefit both parties making them better off than if they produced both the products themselves. A country better at producing both products, would choose to specialize where the gap between its output and that of the other country were greatest. The theory did not predict that countries would benefit equally, they would have to negotiate an exchange rate that was better than the domestic opportunity cost.

There are limitations to this theory. It considered production costs but ignored transport costs and assumed that the products were of equal quality. Trade is influenced by import controls and exchange rate fluctuations. Countries may limit specialization to reduce vulnerability since comparative advantage can change overtime. A lot of world trade is between advanced countries producing different versions of the same product.

see also...

Free Trade and Protectionism; Opportunity Cost

Competition Policy and Contestable Markets

Governments attempt to regulate business activity in order to ensure that it operates in the public interest. The Monopolies and Mergers Commission, now known as the Competition Commission, is the body responsible for investigating how behaviour, such as takeover and merger activity, affects competition. Where a firm, or a group of firms acting together, has 25% or more of total market sales there is a potential for the abuse of market power. Competition policy also involves preventing restrictive practices, such as manufacturers insisting on a minimum retail price. Cartels and agreements to prevent, restrict, or distort competition are also unlawful. Industries that were formerly in state ownership, are all regulated by watchdog bodies, with the power to influence the price that firms charge. The idea behind all competition policy is that competition brings economic benefits. It leads to greater efficiency, lower prices, greater choice and higher product quality. Firms facing actual or potential competitors will, in theory, concentrate on improving their product and lowering their production costs. There are also wider benefits of competition in that if firms are efficient, their international competiveness will improve and the economy will see higher exports, lower imports and more employment. In the past, competition policy has been very pragmatic, each case has been investigated on its own merits. Action against firms has only been taken when it is clear that the disadvantages of their behaviour outweigh the advantages.

One of the problems in promoting competition is the existence of barriers facing new entrants into an industry. A truly contestasee market would be where there was freedom of entry and exit. In theory this occurs in perfect and monopolistic competition.

> ### see also...
> *Perfect Competition; Monopoly; Monopolistic Competition*

Consumer Expenditure

The amount spent on final goods and services represents roughly two thirds of the total expenditure in the circular flow of income. Changes in this variable therefore have a big impact on the level of economic activity. The basic decision consumers make is over the amount that they will spend and save out of their disposable income. Economists use the term *marginal propensity to consume* to describe what consumers will do with any extra income they receive. One of the problems with consumer expenditure is the fraction that is spent on imports. A high marginal propensity to import means that as the standard of living rises, there will be a greater than proportional rise in imports and a deterioration in the balance of trade. Changes in consumption are affected by factors such as expectations; a fall in consumer confidence can suddenly boost savings. Occasionally, changes in wealth can affect current consumption; if the value of assets rises, it can encourage more spending. The pattern of consumer expenditure is influenced by income, tastes and family circumstances. Expenditure data can be obtained from sales figures and the Household Expenditure Survey. As incomes rise, expenditure on basic goods will form a smaller proportion of total spending. The growth products are those which are income elastic or sensitive to income changes. The terms necessities and luxuries are of little use in analysing consumer expenditure because they involve value judgements and what are today's luxuries will probably be tomorrow's necessities.

If the economy is in recession, the government can boost the level of consumption expenditure, by fiscal measures such as a reduction in income tax or indirect taxes. A cut in interest rates would be an appropriate monetary policy because it would discourage saving, encourage borrowing and reduce mortgage payments, which gives consumers more money to spend at their discretion.

see also...

Circular Flow of Income

Cost Benefit Analysis

A cost benefit approach can be applied to any situation where a choice involves gains and losses. Cost benefit analysis was developed as an aid to social decision making by governments. A rational decision on major investment projects must take into account all the different views of people who will be affected by the outcome. In other words, cost benefit analysis is trying to measure the opportunity cost of a decision.

The first step in the analysis is to identify all the possible costs and benefits. The problem is that some of these will only be apparent when the project is completed and operating in the future. Streams of expected future revenue or costs will be worth less than present values because of inflation. They must be discounted to present value in order to integrate them with the other costs and benefits identified. It is difficult to put exact monetary values on costs and benefits. Different people will place different values on events such as noise pollution or environmental damage. The net benefits of a project will simply be the total value of benefits minus the total costs. A project should never go ahead if the social cost exceeds the social benefit. The social cost is simply the private costs on the individuals involved, plus any negative externalities or wider damage to welfare caused by the project. Social benefit includes private gains and positive externalities on third parties.

Cost benefit analysis can be used in any investment decision aimed at improving welfare. It does not guarantee a morally correct or fair decision because value judgements will be made in assessing monetary costs and benefits. A project can only add to welfare if there are gains without anyone being worse off; any losers must be fully compensated for their losses or the decision will be unfair.

see also...

Opportunity Cost; Externalities

Cost Push Inflation

This type of inflation is the result of a fall in the aggregate supply in the economy. In theory, anything that pushes up production costs can trigger price increases. One likely cause of cost push inflation is a rise in the price of imported raw materials because of a change in the world market conditions of demand and supply. Another would be pressure to increase the wages paid to workers. This wage push might be initiated by workers organized in trade unions, or be the result of widespread labour shortages. The motives behind wage demands are either to boost real income or to maintain real income in the face of rising prices. Wage demands that are not accompanied by productivity gains can be inflationary, but the decision to raise prices lies with the producers. Some firms in competitive markets may be reluctant to increase prices in case sales fall by a greater percentage, lowering their sales revenue. If however all other firms are putting prices up, they will join in without harming their market share. If the rise in production costs leads to a reduction in output in the economy, the government may expand the money supply. This will raise aggregate demand and contribute to the inflationary process. Once inflation is under way, there can be a wage-wage spiral, in addition to a wage-price spiral. Workers justifications for higher pay may include comparability with other occupations, or a desire to preserve traditional differentials when pay relative to others has changed.

Once underway, price rises can generate inflationary expectations. People trying to protect their real income will take action that brings about further inflation. Cost push inflation can be triggered by government policy in the form of an increase in indirect taxation or a rise in interest rates which increases the cost of borrowed funds. Some critics of the minimum wage argue that it would have inflationary consequences.

see also...

Demand Pull Inflation; Minimum Wage

Costs of Production

A firm's costs are simply the money value of all the factor inputs to the production process. Though accountants take into account any business costs for which there is a receipt, economists suggest that the true costs must take into account any sacrifices made by the entrepreneur. This gives the concept of a normal profit. It is the minimum level of economic reward necessary to keep the business going, and can be regarded as a cost of production. It is abnormal or supernormal profit that is the reward for risk taking. A firm's costs can be divided into fixed costs or overheads, and variable or direct costs. A *fixed cost* is one that is independent of output whereas a *variable cost* depends directly on the amount produced. Total cost is the sum of fixed cost and variable cost. The most important cost is the cost per unit of output or the average total cost. A firm will only produce if the price or average revenue covers its average total cost. This is a breakeven output and the firm would be making normal profit.

The marginal cost is the addition to the total cost resulting from the production of one extra unit. This will influence a firm's choice of output, and it is assumed that the firm will wish to maximize profits. The output that will guarantee this is where marginal cost equals marginal revenue. Production efficiency will require the firm to produce at lowest unit cost. In the long run, firms will attempt further cost reduction through capital investment that will boost labour productivity and shift average costs downwards. Where fixed cost represents a high proportion of total cost because of research and development costs or the use of expensive fixed capital, they have a big incentive to increase output to raise profits. Firms producing on a larger scale may find that unit costs fall because of what are called *economies of scale*.

see also...

Firms Revenue; Profits and Profit Maximization; Economies of Scale

Crowding Out Theory

This theory criticizes the attempt to boost the economy by expansionary fiscal policy. The suggestion is, that if the government decides to increase its expenditure, it will not have the effect on aggregate demand that was hoped for. It is likely that the extra resources for government spending would damage business investment. If a government is running a *budget deficit*, where spending exceeds tax revenue, then it will have to borrow the money. There is a fixed quantity of savings available at any one time. If the government's demand for borrowed funds rises, it will put upward pressure on the price of those funds, i.e. interest rates will rise. This will reduce the level of business investment, so although the government has spent more, the private spending will be lower, and aggregate demand will not increase much, if at all. Of course the government could avoid this financial crowding out effect by increasing the money supply, but this would trigger demand pull inflation near full employment. If the money was borrowed from abroad, financial crowding out would not occur.

If a government financed higher spending by raising taxes, then consumer spending would fall and this would counteract the effect of extra government injection of money. If extra government spending did lead to interest rates rising, there might be an effect on capital inflows into the economy. This could strengthen the exchange rate, reducing the competitiveness of exports; this might lower aggregate demand. Crowding out of private investment and consumer spending would only really work in an economy where savings were not rising.

Crowding out theory became tied up with the argument that public sector borrowing should be reduced, increasing the resources available for private sector investment.

see also...

Government Borrowing and the National Debt

Deindustrialization

A structural change in the economy is where the composition of the national output changes over a period of time because of the growth of new economic activities. *Industrialization* is a historical process that advanced economies have experienced where fundamentally agricultural economies have been transformed into manufacturing ones. In the British economy, manufacturing itself has seen structural change.

Deindustrialization has been defined in different ways. It refers to the relative and even absolute decline of the manufacturing sector and the growth of the services sector. Manufacturing now accounts for only a quarter of the total output of the economy. The causes of the process are controversial, but central to the problem has been the failure to hold export market share and to prevent the loss of domestic markets to foreign competition.

Deindustrialization is only an economic problem when the economic resources released by the decline of some activities are not taken up by the growth areas. It is for this reason that deindustrialization has played a major part in rising unemployment and regional inequality. It also accounts for the fall in manual and unskilled employment. It partly explains the weakness in the British balance of payments, and the reduction in aggregate demand has had a negative effect on economic growth. Some deindustrialization was inevitable because there is always structural change in any dynamic economy. It is the pace and depth of manufacturing decline in Britain that has been surprising. The solutions to the problem involve *supply-side policies* to encourage those areas of manufacturing with growth potential and to improve competitiveness by increasing labour productivity.

see also...

Economic Growth; International Competitiveness

Demand Pull Inflation

If there is unused capacity in the economy, a rise in total expenditure or aggregate demand will lead to a rise in output. As the economy gets closer to capacity, there may be some shortages and upward pressure on wage levels in the labour market. This will lead to prices as well as output, beginning to rise. Whenever aggregate demand rises faster than the aggregate supply, there will be what is known as demand pull inflation. One important idea was the so-called Phillips relationship. This predicted that the closer to full employment the government chose to run the economy, the faster the rate of inflation would accelerate. There was therefore a trade-off between full employment and the control of inflation.

An increase in aggregate demand can be caused by a rise in consumer expenditure, business investment, government expenditure, or a net injection resulting from export revenue exceeding import expenditure. Monetarists believe that the cause can be traced back to an increase in the money supply in the economy.

For inflation to persist, there must be a continuous rise in aggregate demand. Demand pull inflation is therefore associated with a booming economy where government fiscal and monetary policies are expansionary. It can set off inflationary expectations and workers keen to protect real income can exert wage pressure leading to *cost push inflation*.

The solution to demand pull inflation is to operate a deflationary policy. Appropriate fiscal policies could be a cut in government expenditure or a rise in taxation. A reduction in the money supply or a rise in interest rates would be the preferred monetarist solution. The difficulty is not just finding a solution, but in correctly identifying the cause.

see also...

Fiscal Policy; Monetarism and Monetary Policy

Demerit Goods

These are goods which impose costs on people who are not direct consumers of the product, as well as those who are. In this sense, demerit goods are regarded as being socially harmful. The problem is that free markets will produce anything for which there is an effective demand. The degree of harm done by consuming products is not easily measured and therefore our definition of what makes something a demerit good involves opinion or a value judgement.

The example usually given of a socially harmful product is tobacco. It can cause health damage to users and non-users and there are economic costs associated with these effects. The economic case against smoking is that the market price does not include these costs, with the result that the product is underpriced; this encourages overconsumption. Governments have tried to reduce consumption by raising the supply costs through taxation. This is not very successful in conditions of low price elasticity of demand.

The government is acting in a paternalistic manner, trying to protect users and non-users from the consequences of consumption. It is making the judgement that the social cost is greater than the social benefit. The economic case put forward by consumers is that it interferes with freedom of choice; the contribution in tax revenue more than outweighs the economic cost of the negative effects. If this is true, it could be argued that the activity has net social benefit. Consumption can be reduced by making the product illegal and preventing imports from countries where it is still legal. Alternatively, the government can artificially raise production costs or control the output through a licensing system. The best solution would be to try and shift tastes away from a demerit good, but this is particularly difficult where it has addictive qualities.

see also...
Merit Goods; Cost Benefit Analysis

Development Economics

Over 75% of the world's population live in what have been pessimistically called *less developed*, or optimistically, *developing economies*.

The study of developing economies or underdevelopment recognizes a fundamental difference between the ideas of economic growth and economic development. Economic growth is to do with the rate at which GDP is increasing per head of population. Economic development refers to the growth in the welfare of the population. Growth is not a sufficient condition for development because the distribution of the income is a critical factor in welfare. The trickle down theory, suggesting that rapid economic growth would eliminate poverty, has proved to be a poor explanation of real world events. Some countries show signs of dualism, where a prosperous modern sector exists alongside an agricultural system with people at, or close to, subsistence level.

Development is about the quality of life and the choices that people have. It therefore involves value judgements about what is acceptable. The basic needs approach to development identifies simple targets that must be reached including:

★ adequate food, clothing, shelter and health care;
★ universal access to education and employment;
★ adequate leisure time;
★ political and religious freedom.

Development economics tends to describe the characteristics of developing economies and identifies the obstacles to achieving development. The problem is that developing economies are not all the same, e.g. there is a sub-group that has experienced rapid growth, based in exports, whilst others burdened with debt have seen GDP stagnate.

see also...

Economic Growth; Third World Debt

Direct Taxation

The Government has a choice of taxing income, wealth or consumption to finance its expenditure. A direct tax is a compulsory contribution imposed on the person who is intended to pay. The main forms of direct tax are *income tax* on individuals and *corporation tax* on businesses. Although there is no general tax on the ownership of personal wealth, when property changes hands for more money than it cost the seller, a *capital gains tax* may be incurred, and when property changes hands on the death of the owner, an *inheritance tax* may be incurred.

Income tax dates from the 1790s, and has until recently been the major source of tax revenue. It can be designed to be progressive, proportional or regressive. The idea of a *progressive tax* is to take an increasing proportion in tax as the level of the taxpayers' income rises. This is done by increasing the marginal tax rates. There has been a move away from this idea because it was argued that there were serious disincentive effects on work and risk taking if the economic rewards were highly taxed. There was an idea that a cut in the high marginal rates would actually bring in more revenue from income tax because the incentive to avoid and evade tax would be less. One of the principles of a tax system is that it should be equitable. This means treating people with equal means in the same way. It explains why income generated from any source should be taxed and why gains from the transfer of wealth are taxed. Not all income is taxed however, individuals receive personal allowances and companies can offset some expenditure against tax. Economists see national insurance contributions raised to finance pension and sickness benefit as a direct tax. The burden of the tax is shared between employees, employers and the government.

> ## see also...
> **Indirect Taxation**

Economic Activity Rates

This term refers to the proportion of any age group which participates in the labour market, and is therefore economically active. The age limits chosen for the working population are between 16 and 65. Within this group however are people who are not economically active, through personal choice or circumstances. A proportion of people in the younger section are in full-time education and training. There are individuals unable to participate because of illness and disability or because they are full-time carers of dependants. There will be a relatively small number of individuals with no economic incentive to seek economic activity. The picture of economic activity is complicated by those who are economically active on a part-time basis, both inside and outside the 16–65 age group.

The post-war model of economic activity assumed an activity rate for adult males to be close to 100%. The trend has been for the rate to fall over time because of structural changes in the economy which have affected employment. Redundancies and early retirement are the main causes.

Another major change has been the rise in the economic activity of females. This has coincided with a huge increase in part-time employment, with the services sector of the economy providing the bulk of new employment opportunities. Explanations for higher female economic activity rates emphasize the progress in education together with a change in social attitudes and wage levels.

The government can increase the economic activity rate by:

★ encouraging more employment opportunities for people who have previously been labelled as non-workers;
★ reducing the problem of long-term unemployment;
★ improving the caring services for the dependant groups;
★ encouraging greater flexibility in the conditions of employment.

Economic Growth

Economic growth is the process where there is an increase in the aggregate supply or the productive potential of an economy. It is measured by the annual change in the GDP or the output of the domestic economy. A rise in GDP can be a reflection of the state of the business cycle, in that it rises during recovery and falls during a recession. True growth is therefore best measured from peak to peak in the business cycle, to show that the increase in GDP is due to an economy shifting to new production possibilities. The basic sources of economic growth are an increase in the quantity of factors of production or a rise in their productivity. Economic growth is a cumulative process. A 3% annual growth rate will raise GDP by 10% in three years, double it in 24 years, and quadruple it in 48 years. It is easier for countries with a lower base level of GDP to raise its growth rate than it is for rich countries, but the truth is that a lot of countries face severe barriers in their quest for it.

The exact causes of growth are controversial and there are numerous growth theories offering explanations. Any country wishing to raise its growth rate will have to increase capital accumulation and investment. Human capital and an increase in the stock of knowledge through education and training, is now seen as a much more important factor in growth than previously, because of the importance of technology in the fortunes of business enterprise. In government economic policy there has been increasing emphasis on what is called *supply side economics*. Some people see intervention as a positive force for growth while others prefer supply side policies which involve less government intervention. One of the difficulties with any policy aimed at promoting growth is that it might damage the other macroeconomic objectives in the short term.

see also...

Supply Side Policies; Development Economics

Economic Systems

The fundamental objective of any economic system is to get the maximum use from scarce resources. Economists use the term *optimum allocation of resources* to describe an efficient outcome. An economic system is simply the organization that is chosen to achieve the ends. The basic decisions which must be made by any economic system are:

★ what goods and services will be produced;
★ how will the output be made;
★ how will the output be distributed.

The choice of economic systems is political and involves value judgements. They exist in a spectrum ranging from socialism at one extreme to capitalism at the other. In a socialist system there would be state ownership of all the resources and the questions would be answered by state administration. In a capitalist system, there would be privately owned property which individuals could choose to use in the production system. Resources in this model are allocated by the free interaction of the market forces of demand and supply with a minimal amount of government intervention in the way the economy functions. All economic systems in the world are now described as mixed, in that they have elements of both systems. Disadvantages exist in the form of inefficiences in the socialist system; inequality and unacceptable products in the capitalist system.

Mixed economies differ in the degree of state intervention, measured by the proportion of total resources accounted for by government and the type of intervention. The choice here is basically between physical rationing of resources through legislation and regulation, or intervening in the price mechanism via economic incentives such as taxation and subsidies.

see also...

Transition Economies

Economies of Scale

In the short run, a firm may try to be productively efficient by producing at the lowest point of its average cost curve. In the long run it may choose to operate on a larger scale. If the output increases by more than the inputs, the firm will experience increasing returns to scale. An economy of scale is the benefit a firm receives in the form of a reduction in long run unit cost as a result of its increased size. An internal economy is a benefit that each firm gets as a result of its own growth. When a firm has exploited all the internal economies and is operating at the minimum efficient scale where long run unit cost is lowest, it can still get benefit from external economies. An *external economy* benefits all firms in an expanding industry, particularly where it is highly localized. Examples may be improvements in transport infrastructure, a pool of specialized labour, cooperation in research and development and local training programmes.

In manufacturing, technical economies can occur because the growth in output beyond a certain point makes new production techniques economic. Fuller use can be made of expensive fixed capital. There may be managerial economies through the employment of specialist staff and cost savings based on accumulated experience of organizing production. Marketing economies can occur through the bulk buying of materials or in the distribution of the finished product. Large firms can get greater access to loans at a lower cost because lenders see them as a lower risk. Diversification can be an economy of scale because it allows the firm to spread business risks. Widening the product range is sometimes called an *economy of scope*. It is possible for a firm to grow too big, managerial diseconomies can result from coordination problems within complex organizations. External diseconomies can arise out of the clustering of growth activities in a particular location.

see also...

Costs of Production

Efficiency

The objective of any economic system is to maximize the use of scarce resources and to allocate them to different uses in an efficient way. All the production units should operate at their lowest unit cost. This would be a suitable definition of *productive efficiency* for firms. Of course, dynamic firms will be investing in production methods that reduce the unit cost over time, in order to boost their total profit. It follows from this, that the most efficient output will be where the firm produces at the minimum point of the long run average cost curve. In terms of the whole economy, productive efficiency would be where there is no unemployment of resources and production possibilities are maximized. *Allocative efficiency* is where the market price reflects the producer's marginal cost, giving an acceptable profit, while also reflecting the marginal utility or the satisfaction the consumer receives from purchasing the last unit. Any firm selling at a price higher than marginal cost would be described as *allocatively inefficient.*

If there were perfect competition in all markets then the whole economy would be economically efficient. Productive efficiency would coincide with allocative efficiency. Market imperfections mean that allocative and productive efficiency are not always achieved and the resulting market failure involves a loss of welfare. An additional problem is that there may be a conflict between equity and efficiency. This means that although an economy may be economically efficient, it is not necessarily equitable or fair to different groups of people. Any attempt to improve the welfare of one group, by changing the allocation of resources in an efficient economy, will automatically be at the expense of another group. This is often called *Pareto efficiency* after the Italian economist Vilfredo Pareto (1848–1923) who pioneered the study of efficiency. In assessing how well an economy works, it is inevitable that economists will make value judgements; this branch of economic study is called *welfare economics.*

Elasticity

The term elasticity in economic analysis means responsiveness to a change. In the case of *price elasticity of demand* it is the response of consumers to a change in the price of the product. A change in the supply conditions in a market can cause a new equilibrium price to be made. If the change in quantity demanded is less than the price change, it illustrates low price elasticity or a relatively price inelastic demand curve. Products with low price elasticity make ideal targets for indirect taxation if the government wants to raise revenue.

A lack of close substitutes and high priority given to the product by consumers will lead to a low price elasticity. A firm facing low price elasticity can increase its total revenue by raising the price; and when demand is price elastic, a price reduction will increase sales revenue. The demand for one product can be sensitive to a change in the price of a related one, known as *cross price elasticity of demand*. If there is a relationship between two products, it is either that they are substitutes or rival products, or complements – where one is required for the other one to work and give consumer satisfaction.

Income elasticity of demand is where sales are sensitive to income changes. Growth products in the economy have high income elasticity of demand. The high income elasticity of demand for imports creates potential balance of payments problems when there is economic growth.

If the demand conditions cause a new equilibrium market price to be established, the *price elasticity of supply* shows how producers respond to this new information. For some products, there is a fixed supply in the short run and the supply is perfectly inelastic. The easier it is to adjust production, the more elastic the supply curve will be.

see also...
Market Mechanism

Entrepreneurship

Like many other ideas in economics, this concept can be defined in different ways. Entrepreneurs are people who undertake a business project. This will involve both risk taking and the management of economic resources. Most definitions focus on the risk-taking aspect, because successful entrepreneurs often employ other people to carry out the day-to-day running of a business. Enterprise is also defined as the quality of being able to spot business opportunities. Entrepreneurs are therefore usually innovators in dynamic markets. Innovation is the application of new ideas, either in the way resources are used, or with the introduction of new products to the market. Business risks exist because of the uncertainties surrounding a system where production takes place in anticipation of demand. The risk the entrepreneur takes is with the financial capital of the business. It may be the entrepreneur's own money borrowed from financial institutions, or funds belonging to shareholders.

Economic theory assumes that the motivation for taking business risks is the prospect of a surplus of revenue over costs. Entrepreneurs will seek to maximize this amount of abnormal profit. The prospect of profit is what attracts new entrants into an industry, so long as the barriers to entry can be overcome. This is also part of the skill of entrepreneurs.

It is wrong to think that profit is the only motivating factor. Successful entrepreneurs can amass a large stock of personal wealth and it may be the excitement and satisfaction from the challenge that provides their drive. Explanations of the characteristics and motivations of entrepreneurs lie in the field of psychology rather than economics. Teaching management skills and the techniques of business enterprise is itself a growth industry.

see also...

Factors of Production; Profits and Profit Maximization; Firms' Objectives

Environmental Economics

Environmental problems can occur either through the way we choose to manufacture goods or through the consumption of goods and services. Green economics is an attempt to find the most cost effective solutions to current environmental problems.

Environmental damage is the result of market failure. The problem is that the market price does not always reflect the true costs of production. Costs imposed on people other than the producer, e.g. pollution of the environment, are termed *negative externalities*. If these costs are not taken into account then the resulting products are artificially cheap, and this encourages the consumption of the product. The *social cost* of any activity is the private cost plus any negative externalities. The *social benefit* is the private benefit plus any positive externalities. The socially efficient output is where the marginal social benefit equals the marginal social cost.

Environmental economics is the study of how to get the best outcome through legislation or by creating economic incentives for producers and consumers to change their behaviour. Green taxes are one attempt to do this. They are specifically designed to reduce environmental damage rather than to raise revenue, e.g. tax on the burning of fossil fuels or a landfill tax. Furthermore, there is intended to be a link between revenue collected and environmental improvement. This is the idea of earmarked taxes. For example taxes on cars, or the less environmentally friendly fuels, could be introduced to reduce car use, therefore reducing pollution and traffic congestion. The revenue can be used directly to finance or subsidise transport alternatives which have a lower social cost.

see also...

Externalities

Equilibrium

The dictionary definition of equilibrium is a *state of balance or recovery after a disturbance*. The idea of equilibrium in economics appears in both micro- and macro economics. In the market mechanism, the equilibrium price is one where there is no surplus of supply over demand or shortage of demand relative to supply, and is the market clearing price. The equilibrium price is a unique one, which satisfies the producer because it covers the marginal cost of the last unit of output and reflects the price the consumer is willing to pay. The equilibrium price will only change if the conditions of supply and demand alter. Real world markets are dynamic and are in the process of moving from one equilibrium to another. A market can be in *disequilibrium* because of some imperfection or intervention, such as the minimum wage legislation or as a result of the CAP.

In macroeconomics, the term equilibrium is used to describe the level of income and employment that results from the actual level of aggregate expenditure. Changes in the components of aggregate demand or shifts in aggregate supply, will always take the economy to a new equilibrium. Equilibrium does *not* imply that it is efficient or desirable. The target for macroeconomic equilibrium would be the level of full employment income, or one that does not damage the other macroeconomic objectives. One of these objectives is a balance of payments equilibrium where the inflows of money into the economy exactly match the value of outflows.

In the circular flow of income, the equilibrium national income will be where the value of injections into the flow, i.e. investment plus government spending plus exports, is exactly balanced by the leakages, i.e. savings plus taxes plus imports. There will be no tendency for the national income to change unless consumer expenditure or any of these six variables change, taking the economy on an upward or downward path.

EU and the EURO

The European Union has 15 members. Eleven of them are part of the EMU that was established in 1999, and will be in full economic and monetary union by 2002, when their national currencies will be replaced by the single currency called the EURO. The British government has decided to join in principle when certain conditions are fulfilled and it is convinced that the single currency will be in the economy's best interests. This decision will be controversial, because it will be difficult to establish if the benefits outweigh the costs. It is not just an economic issue; full union has always been a political objective. Supporters believe that a unified Europe will guarantee peace and give the European zone more influence in world affairs. Critics regard this as a stage too far in the historical process of greater integration and would prefer that it stopped at the EU being a single economic market.

The decision to encourage wider membership of the EU is also controversial. There are about 12 potential new members. Some economists argue that it will be difficult to manage a large diverse group of economies with a single interest rate.

In the EMU, the responsibility for macroeconomic management lies with the ECB, an independent central bank. Its objective is to get an inflation rate below 2% each year in the European zone. The instrument for achieving this is monetary policy, in the form of interest rate changes. National governments will still have some discretion over fiscal policy, but some observers think that harmonization of taxes within EMU will reduce this. Critics wonder what economic tools a national government will be left with if their economy is in recession when the others are not, since budget deficits are limited to 3% of GDP.

The EU is reaching the final stages of its evolution, in what will turn out to have been a major economic and political experiment.

Exchange Rates

The exchange rate is the price of one currency in terms of another. Like any price it is determined by demand and supply. Changes in the market conditions will lead to a currency appreciating or depreciating in a free market. The main participants in foreign exchange markets are end users such as businesses and tourists but central banks may also influence the current exchange rate. The market is also influenced by the market makers who hold stocks of foreign currencies. There are also speculators and people who make a profit by transferring money between currencies. An economy can choose between fixed exchange rates that can only be altered by agreement with trading partners, or floating rates determined by the strength of demand and supply. In the past, dissatisfaction with both systems led to managed exchange rates, where the Bank of England maintained the pound at a level that the government thought appropriate.

It is difficult to tell what the best value of the pound is, because a low exchange rate makes imports dearer in terms of pounds and can add to inflation, while a strong pound can damage exporters and employment.

In the foreign exchange market, the demand for pounds is the same thing as the supply of foreign currency and vice versa. The trade in goods and services is a big influence on the value of the pound, e.g. a fall in exports will lower the demand for pounds and its value will fall. One of the important things to recognize is that changes in the exchange rate also influence the level of imports and exports. Inflows of investment money from abroad will strengthen the pound, while any outflows will weaken it.

If Britain joins the EMU, the government will no longer be able to lower the exchange rate in order to increase the competitiveness of British exports. Exchange rates will cease to be an economic objective or a tool of macroeconomic management.

Externalities

In economics, externalities are third party effects or spillover effects. They are the costs or benefits experienced by people not directly involved in the market activity as producers or consumers. Externalities may be positive (benefits) or negative (costs). In a perfect market these would be taken into account by the price. Market failure is therefore where the price only takes into account the private cost to the producer and the private benefit to the consumer.

Pollution is the usual example of negative externalities in the production of goods. The social cost of the output would be the private costs of production plus a value for the harm done to everyone as a consequence of the production decision.

If the market price only reflects the private cost and benefit, then it is underpricing the good and this artificially encourages higher consumption than would occur in an efficient market. The solution to this type of market failure is to somehow internalize the external cost. This can be done by imposing a tax on the polluter equal to the value of the negative externalities. The *social optimum price* will be one where the *marginal social cost* of an activity is equal to the *marginal social benefit*. When there are positive externalities from the production or consumption of something, the *marginal social benefit* is greater than the *marginal private benefit*. The price will lead to this merit good being underconsumed. An appropriate correction for this market failure would be a subsidy paid to either the producer or the consumer. Externalities justify government intervention in the particular activity to encourage or discourage it. The intervention can take the form of economic incentives to persuade people to change their behaviour or regulations which force them to change. Sometimes the political cost is an explanation for governments' reluctance to intervene. If traffic congestion and pollution are economic problems why has the government not imposed high taxation or regulations on motorists?

Factors of Production

This is the collective term for the *economic resources* in the *production system*. It is these inputs that are transformed into the output of final goods and services. Economists group the resources into four categories.

Land is the term for all natural resources that are used in production. Raw materials are therefore taken from the stock of natural assets. The economic reward that goes to the owners of this factor of production is called *rent*.

Labour can be defined as the sum of all the physical and mental effort that goes into production and includes the tasks of management. The economic return to those who supply labour is *wages*. An artificial distinction is sometimes made between wages paid weekly and salaries paid in monthly instalments.

Capital is the economic term for any *man-made productive asset*. It is business capital that is the factor of production rather than personal or social capital.

Business capital refers to the physical capital equipment and property of firms. The economic reward to capital is called *interest*.

Enterprise is regarded as the coordinating factor of production. It involves both the organization of the economic resources and an element of risk taking, its reward is *profit*.

The term *factor productivity* is used in an attempt to measure the exact contribution of factors to the final value of output. Labour productivity is measured in terms of output per head. The contribution of each worker to the final value is called the *marginal revenue product* and, in theory, forms the basis of wage payments. Factor prices and productivity influence whether firms are capital or labour intensive in their search for the least cost factor combination.

---

see also...

Costs of Production

Firms' Objectives

The standard assumption in the economic theory of the firm is that *each firm will seek to maximize profits*. This gives a unique prediction about the firm's output. Any profit-maximizing firm will produce up to the point where the cost of making the last unit is equal to the revenue received from it where MC = MR. To produce below this would mean sacrificing potential profit, because each successive unit is bringing in more revenue than it cost to make. To go beyond this implies marginal cost being greater than marginal revenue, reducing total profit. In real world firms, it may not be possible to recognize this output or there may be objectives other than profit maximization; the way firms are organized can affect objectives; there may be several goals and they may conflict. The firm may be forced to compromise in order to keep the stakeholders happy.

A firm may prefer to set objectives in terms of sales. It could go for sales maximization consistent with just covering cost, in order to break into a new market or increase market share. Sales revenue maximisation would appeal to management if their economic rewards were directly linked to growth in the value of sales. Other managerial objectives include better working conditions and greater non-monetary rewards. It is assumed that the owners of business are most interested in profit, but small owner operators may have different priorities, e.g. work satisfaction, leisure time, altruism, or the employment of family members.

Firms' objectives and behaviour may be influenced by market structure. In oligopolistic markets dominated by a handful of large firms, it may be too risky to try to maximize revenue or profits because of rivals' reactions. This has led to the theory of satisficing where the firm aims for enough profit to keep shareholders happy, high wages to satisfy the workforce, and reasonable prices to retain customers.

see also...

Profits and Profit Maximization;
Entrepreneurship

Firms' Revenue

A firm's sales revenue is the price obtained for each unit multiplied by the number of units sold. In economic theory, there are two possible revenue situations facing firms. The first is where the firm can sell as much as it can produce at the ruling market price. The firm's demand curve, average revenue and marginal revenue are the same thing. The demand curve would be horizontal, occurring when there is perfect competition. The second and more realistic situation is where firms face some kind of downward sloping demand curve. The firm can only increase sales volume by lowering the price. The demand is still equal to average revenue, but the marginal revenue will be less than average revenue.

Sales revenue maximization is a possible objective of the firm. If sales are increased to the point where marginal revenue or the revenue obtained from the last unit is zero, then the firm will have maximized its total revenue. There will still be abnormal profit as long as the total revenue exceeds the total cost. There is an important link between cost and revenue. If competitive firms have lower costs than their rivals, a price reduction to increase sales volume can be made without sacrificing profit. A price war may be started as a strategy to squeeze higher cost rivals out of the market. Some firms could actually operate with revenue below costs, if they are able to use the profits from other branches of economic activity. This principle is known as *cross subsidization*.

Firms with monopoly power may raise the price in order to boost revenue. They could also experiment with *price discrimination*, charging different prices to different groups of customers. All firms will hope to boost their revenue by permanently shifting the demand curve to the right, by product innovation, or through a combination of marketing techniques.

see also...

Firms' Objectives; Monopoly

Fiscal Policy

Fiscal policy can be defined as anything to do with government expenditure and taxation. It is mainly used to influence the level of aggregate expenditure and therefore the level of income and employment in the economy.

If the government wants to raise aggregate demand, it can reduce taxes or increase its own expenditure. This implies that it would be operating a budget deficit – an appropriate policy if the economy were in recession. The expansionary action will not automatically raise total spending because it could be outweighed by a fall in consumer expenditure, investment, or a deficit in the current account of the balance of payments. When a government cuts taxes it will not automatically boost spending because consumers may decide to save their extra disposable income rather than spend it.

A *deflationary fiscal policy* can be used to take money out of the circular flow if aggregate spending threatens to outstrip production and therefore cause inflationary pressure. Fiscal policy can be used to achieve other objectives such as income redistribution in order to reduce absolute or relative poverty. It can also operate on aggregate supply by giving tax incentives or grants to labour or capital to improve the efficiency with which resources are used.

Fiscal measures can be used to deal with production and comsumption externalities.

Fiscal policy can have an opportunity cost in that measures taken to reach one objective can damage another. An increase in taxation and a cut in government spending might reduce demans pull inflation, but can increase unemployment. Along monetary policy, fiscal policy is the major tool of economic management.

---

see also...

Aggregate Demand; Monetary Policy; Opportunity Cost

Free Trade and Protectionism

Economic theory predicts that free trade between nations works to increase economic welfare. Some countries can produce goods and services with less resources than others, and are described as having *absolute advantage*. Even where this occurs, it is still possible for countries to gain from specialization and trade. As long as the relative efficiency with which goods and services can be produced differs between countries, each can specialize in the product where it has greatest *comparative advantage*. Countries will find that they can increase the variety of products available to the population and are better off than they would be on their own. The gains from trade depend on the exchange rate. Changes in the demand for and supply of the goods and services will alter this rate.

There are disadvantages to free trade. Narrow specialization can make an economy vulnerable and comparative advantage can change over time. Relative advantages in production can be offset by transport costs.

Protectionism may be justified in particular conditions, to help an infant industry develop or to counter unfair competition. The EU is an example where there is free trade between members, but taxes are imposed on imports from non-members. Protectionist measures may take the form of tariffs on imports to artificially raise import prices to domestic price levels. Another option is to put physical restrictions on the volume of goods imported. Administrative regulations and exchange controls on currency can also limit trade. Protectionism can also include subsidising export prices.

Erecting barriers to trade is unlikely to solve a balance of payments deficit because competitive retaliation by others will reduce the country's exports. Protectionism can have a high social cost. The long run solution must be to use supply side policies that will raise productivity and make domestic goods more competitive internationally. This will increase exports, and reduce imports, at the same time.

Full Employment and Types of Unemployment

In the 1944 White Paper on Employment, the government made a commitment to the idea of full employment, and it has been an ideal ever since.

Data on unemployment can be obtained in two ways: official statistics use the *claimant count for benefits* such as jobseekers allowance; the International Labour Office (ILO) uses *surveys*. The ILO defines unemployment as the number of people who have been actively seeking work in the four weeks before, and those about to start work or who are available for work in the two weeks following, the survey. Full employment would be a situation where everyone who was seeking work would be successful in finding it. Zero unemployment is highly unlikely, because there will always be some transitional unemployment where people are between jobs. It is also difficult to eliminate some of the other causes of unemployment. For this reason, government objectives for employment tend to be presented in a less precise way. Phrases such as a *high* and *stable level of employment* are preferred to full employment. In the past, full employment has also been interpreted as the level of employment consistent with achieving the other macroeconomic objectives. Apart from *transitional and seasonal unemployment,* which are traditional and minor causes of unemployment, there are others which pose more of a problem. *Frictional unemployment* can occur even when there are unfilled vacancies in the labour market. This kind of unemployment is simply a mismatch between the demand for labour and the available supply. People may not fill vacancies because of occupational or geographic immobility. *Structural unemployment* results from a fall in the demand for particular products. In Britain, the growth of the service sector has not taken up all the labour released through the decline of manufacturing. *Technological unemployment* is a variation of the structural problem. When capital is substituted for labour there can be some short-term and even long-term unemployment as a direct consequence.

Globalization

This is an example of an idea that is being used in different contexts. To an economist, globalization is a process in which individual national economies have increased their links with others, leading to greater interdependence and yet increasing competition at the same time. This complex interaction has an impact on national economies. The available tools of economic management may not be sufficient for governments to solve the domestic problems that result from the interactions.

The elements of globalization are the growth in world trade in goods and services, the increase in direct foreign investment and technology transfer between economies. The availability of global finance, falling transport costs, lower trade barriers and instant communication have all encouraged firms to operate across national boundaries. At the heart of the process is the restructuring of firms, allowing them to reallocate production resources to countries where there are cost advantages or markets showing signs of rapid growth.

Increased trade and investment in other economies is also accompanied by increased imports and greater foreign ownership of productive resources in any national economy. This result of globalization gives rise to tensions when the two flows are not equal. Globalization, driven by market forces, does not guarantee that participants will benefit equally from increased prosperity. Some of the newly industrializing economies saw short-term economic crises or slowdowns in their rate of growth in the 1990s.

Globalization may bring with it some job destruction in individual economies, and greater job insecurity as business capital becomes more mobile. It can lead to downward pressure on wages particularly those for less skilled workers. Downturns in economic activity in parts of the world economy will be quickly transmitted to all national economies. One of the biggest challenges of globalization will be to obtain sufficient international cooperation to maintain economic stability in the whole system in the interest of all national economies.

Government Borrowing and the National Debt

Governments have several ways of financing their expenditure. The main one is taxation or through direct charges for the provision of certain services. The less likely options are borrowing, and increasing the amount of money in existence. Borrowing can never be a permanent option because it is postponing a financial problem. It also carries a cost in the interest that has to be paid on the loans and this will be a burden on taxpayers.

Borrowing is associated with the decision to operate budget deficits. This may be a deliberate policy or a result of an economic recession. The term for this shortfall and any borrowing by local authorities and state owned business is the public sector borrowing requirement (PSBR). A budget surplus would provide an opportunity to pay off some past debt, hence the term public sector debt repayment (PSDR). Governments have been determined to reduce borrowing as a proportion of GDP. The national debt is simply the accumulation of all the governments past borrowing. Overall the Labour government aims to keep the total public sector debt in any year to below 40% of GDP. Money borrowed from abroad will be a problem because the interest and repayment will represent an outflow of resources. When money is borrowed from inside the economy, it is merely a redistribution of income from taxpayers to the debt holders. The present government believes that borrowing should only be done to finance investment projects within the public sector.

Current spending should be matched by tax revenue over the course of the business cycle, implying zero budget deficits. Any temporary deficit is now called the public sector net cash requirement (PSNCR) If Britain joins the EMU system its borrowing would be limited anyway. High borrowing is not a sensible way to finance public expenditure, but the decision to repay accumulated debt as a major priority is controversial.

Government Expenditure

Discussion of government expenditure is linked with views about the economic role of a government in a mixed economy and is heavily influenced by the rise in public expectations. General government expenditure involves spending on goods, services, interest payments and transfer payments. About 40% of this spending is on what are called *social protection measures* to increase the welfare of less fortunate groups in society. Often, a distinction between current spending on goods and services and capital expenditure on equipment and buildings is made. The biggest item of current spending will be the salary bill for public sector employees. One of the dilemmas facing any government is the opportunity cost of decisions to increase spending on particular programmes, such as health and education. If the growth in spending is higher than the overall growth rate in the economy there are two consequences. The government could take the extra resources from other spending programmes or raise the level of taxation, both of which are politically unpopular. Capital expenditure can be financed from previous budget surpluses or by borrowing. Another option is through partnerships with private sector firms that will expect an economic return on their investment.

Historically, the trend has been for total government expenditure to rise in real terms over time, but some expenditure is outside the government's control. An example is when the economy is in recession. The bill for certain benefits will rise, and at the same time, the yield from taxation will be falling. To some extent these events act as automatic stabilizers, reducing the severity of the economic downturn.

Political parties differ over the total amount and the pattern of government expenditure, but another controversial aspect of government expenditure concerns the efficiency with which services are delivered. One idea is that government should finance services but that the provision could be done by private sector firms which would have an economic incentive to increase efficiency.

Gross National Product

Gross domestic product (GDP) is the monetary value of all the goods and services produced in the domestic economy in the course of one year, regardless of the ownership of the output. Gross *national* product (GNP) is a measure of all the income generated by an economy's resources from inside *and* outside the country on an annual basis: it is GDP plus net property income from abroad. It can be calculated using the expenditure method in national income accounting. The expenditure of consumers and firms' expenditure on investment is added to government expenditure on goods and services and net exports, i.e. the value of exports minus the import value, plus any net property income from abroad. This can give a misleading impression because expenditure flows are valued at market prices which do not always reflect the true factor cost of the product. To convert GNP *at market prices* to GNP at *factor cost*, indirect taxation must be deducted and any subsidies on products must be added.

Sometimes the term *net national product* is used. This is simply GNP minus an allowance for the depreciation or capital consumption of assets used up in the production process. NNP is perhaps the truest guide to the national income that has been generated by an economy.

GNP data is used as the first step in the attempt to measure the standard of living and make international comparisons. Even when it has been refined to GNP per head of population in real terms after taking inflation into account, it is still not a close guide to economic welfare. This is because much depends on how the national income is distributed, the role of the government and working conditions. However, the idea is that it is better to have an imperfect measure than no measure at all. International comparisons are difficult if the GNP is not calculated in the same way nor expressed in a common currency.

Health Economics

Health is a basic component of living standards. In economic terms, it can be seen as an investment good that will improve the quality of *human capital* and therefore contribute to economic growth and higher levels of employment. It is a *merit good* in that good health must be encouraged because of its positive externalities.

The National Health Service highlights the basic economic problem of scarcity. At any one time, the supply of health resources is fixed, while the demand for health services is growing with time. If the health service were regarded as a free market good, the result would be a rise in the price; the consumers most willing and able to pay would get the treatment. When it is provided for everyone regardless of means, there is no price and treatment is rationed through waiting lists.

Health economics investigates the ways of limiting demand and how the efficiency of the service can be increased. One step is to determine the exact labour and material costs for every kind of treatment. The idea then, is to compare different kinds of treatment in terms of cost and expected benefit or outcome. Resources can then be concentrated where the greatest net benefit is obtained. Medical decisions over treatment are bound to have an opportunity cost. A single complex heart operation can use resources that could supply a number of minor operations, improving the quality of life for a large number of patients. The danger is, that value judgements creep in if certain illnesses and patients are considered more important than others. One of the problems in heath economics is the pace of technical progress as new forms of treatment may be very expensive. Medical progress makes more treatment possible, but the treatment costs add to the funding problem. Some capital equipment is now financed through charitable contributions.

Horizontal, Vertical and Lateral Integration

The process of business integration takes place through *takeovers* and *mergers*. It represents external growth as opposed to internal growth via the investment of retained profit. The effect of integration is to concentrate business ownership into fewer hands. *Horizontal integration* occurs between firms in the same stage of the production process. One manufacturer may take over or amalgamate with another making the same product. The difference between a takeover and a merger is that the former involves an attempt to buy out the existing shareholders to get control of the business. A merger implies that both businesses see the advantages of integration. The motives for horizontal integration may be to achieve cost savings and greater efficiency through economies of scale or to get more market power and therefore raise profits.

Vertical integration occurs between firms at different stages of production, so a manufacturer may take over or merge with a supplier of raw materials in backward vertical integration or a retailer in forward integration. The motives here may be to do with security of supply, capturing profit margins or increasing market power.

The term *lateral integration* was intended to describe horizontal integration between firms making different products but where there was some connection either in production techniques or the finished product itself. Hence, an entertainment corporation may wish to go into the travel and hotel industry. There is now plenty of evidence of integration between firms where there are no connections. Takeover and merger activity occurs between diversified organizations hence the label *conglomerate mergers*. Integration sometimes fails to deliver the expected benefits and the problems of managing large business has led to some disintegration and demerger activity. There is considerable discussion on the theme of whether or not integration is in the public interest. The Competition Commission will monitor this activity, attempting to investigate each case on its own merits.

Income and Wealth

In economic terminology, income is defined as a *flow of money over a period of time*. Wealth, on the other hand, is a *stock of accumulated assets at any point in time*. Household income must be ultimately derived from the production of goods and services. The major source of income will be from employment and self-employment. For some, income is in the form of state benefits or what economists call transfer payments. For others, part of their income may come from a return on savings or the use of their property in the production system. Finally, there is a flow of occupational pension income. There is an important distinction between gross income and net income. Net income is gross income minus taxes plus transfer payments. In reality this becomes the household's disposable income.

Saving is the act of converting part of a present flow of income into future consumption spending. Most savings take the form of assets such as bank and building society accounts, stocks and shares, pensions and life assurance contributions or premium bonds.

Savings provide the fund from which firms and the government can borrow to increase the amount of physical capital in the economy, so the wealth of any economy is the total value of the accumulated wealth of households, firms and government.

For most people, the stock of personal assets or wealth is derived from their flow of income. The biggest single asset is likely to be housing wealth, with inheritance playing a significant part in its accumulation. There is a positive correlation between income, wealth accumulation and age. The government can encourage wealth accumulation through tax incentives on saving. While all governments have taxed income, there has been a reluctance to introduce a wealth tax as a way of reducing the degree of inequality between households.

Indirect Taxation

Indirect taxes are imposed on certain products or services that people buy. The main ones are value added tax and excise duties. Apart from raising tax revenue, the purpose of the taxes is to influence consumer expenditure patterns, and to remove money from the circular flow of income. It is the producer who pays the tax revenue to the government, but the burden of the tax is intended to be on the consumer. VAT is an *ad valorum* tax levied on the selling price of chosen goods and services. Some products such as food and exports are exempt, while domestic fuel is taxed at a lower rate than other items. The excise duties imposed on the domestic production of tobacco, alcohol, and hydrocarbon oils, are big revenue raisers for the Exchequer because they all have a low price elasticity of demand. The lack of substitutes means that a rise in price will trigger only a small reduction in consumption, hence taxes on these goods have been regularly increased. Other indirect taxes include the council tax and duties on betting and gaming.

Indirect taxes tend to have a regressive effect in that they take a bigger proportion of the income of people at the lower end of the income distribution.

Taxes on expenditure are becoming more important in the tax system because of the disadvantages that arise from taxing income. Pressure to increase government expenditure has led to a search for new taxes, examples being the insurance premiums tax and the airport departure tax. Some people argue for a more direct link between specific taxes and particular items of government expenditure. For example, taxes from motorists could be spent on roads and the transport system, while the tax from alcohol and tobacco could be spent on the National Health Service. This is called *hypothecation*, but it is impossible to match all individual taxes with particular spending programmes.

Inflation: Meaning and Measurement

nflation is a *process* rather than an economic event. It is defined as a persistent rise in the general level of prices. The rate at which prices change varies over time, a fall in the inflation rate meaning that prices are rising more slowly than before. Inflation does not mean that all prices within the economy are rising, or that they are rising at the same rate. *Creeping inflation* refers to low single-digit inflation rates, while *hyperinflation* suggests a runaway increase in prices.

The alternative way of looking at inflation is that it represents a fall in the internal purchasing power of the currency, because inflation implies that an existing stock of money depreciating in value.

Inflation is measured by using a retail price index (RPI). The notional basket of goods valued in a base year is intended to be representative of the kind of things that most consumers buy, and the price change of each item is weighted to reflect its relative importance to the consumer. Both the goods and the weights need to be updated in line with changes in consumer expenditure patterns.

Changes in the whole RPI from the base period give what is known as the headline rate of inflation. The underlying, or core rate of inflation, is the RPI minus mortgage interest payments, council tax and petrol prices. The RPI is used as a cost of living index in wage negotiations and by the government when deciding on increases in pensions and other benefits.

Other price indexes try to show what is happening to costs and prices in domestic manufacturing. Changes in the producers' input costs feed through into retail prices within a year. The GDP deflator is an index of all the prices in the economy excluding imports. It is used to convert money GDP into real GDP in order to measure change in the volume of output over time.

> *see also...*
>
> **Real and Monetary Values**

Injections and Leakages

The equilibrium level of income in the economy can be determined in two ways. Ultimately, the level of aggregate expenditure, or aggregate demand, must be equal to income. *Equilibrium income* will be the sum of all the components of expenditure, and if any of these change, there will be a new equilibrium. For the circular flow to be in equilibrium, the total inflows must equal the total outflows. An injection is defined as any *money added to the circular flow*. Injections include business investment (I), government expenditure on goods and services (G) and export revenue (X). A leakage is any *income paid out by the production system but not returned to it* through consumer expenditure. The withdrawals or leakages are savings (S), imports (M) and taxation (T). Equilibrium is where:

$$I+G+X = S+M+T.$$

The injections and leakages are determined by different groups of people, and it is highly unlikely that they will always match. This explains some fluctuation in economic activity over time. If the level of injections is higher than the leakages then there will be a rise in the level of income until sufficient extra leakages have been generated to match the level of injections. If the money leaking out is greater than the inflow, then equilibrium income will fall.

It follows from this analysis, that the government can manipulate leakages and injections to influence the total flow of income in the economy in order to get a more acceptable equilibrium. If the objective is to increase income and employment, then the appropriate policy would be to raise the level of injections and reduce the leakages through a combination of fiscal and monetary measures. The flow of consumer expenditure – the largest component of aggregate expenditure – can also be manipulated. It is the inflows and outflows in aggregate expenditure that play a big part in whether the economy is in boom or bust; therefore they affect unemployment and the growth rate.

Innovation

Innovation is the application of new knowledge and understanding to aspects of the production system. Knowledge is now seen as the key economic resource in the search for faster economic growth. There are two specific types of innovation. *Process innovation* is where changes are made in the way that goods and services are produced. In manufacturing, this usually means that the production becomes more capital intensive, using computer controlled machinery rather than labour to produce goods. The increased use of technology can reduce unit costs through increasing labour productivity. Innovation can also be applied to management techniques that can further increase productive efficiency.

Product innovation is where firms redesign existing products in order to increase their utility or satisfaction to customers. This added value can increase a firm's market share and give a boost to the sales of products that have reached maturity in their life cycle. Innovation can also take the form of completely new products. Both kinds of product innovation lead to a response by rivals, but if a firm maintains its competitive edge and manages to reduce costs, then innovation will increase total profits.

Research and development has therefore become a major investment activity by firms and the high cost of this has led to greater cooperation between rivals. There is a strong case for governments to increase spending on research because of the considerable positive externalities as well as private benefits that it brings. Technology and innovation have implications for education spending in general. More knowledge is being transferred across national boundaries with direct inward investment by innovating firms; this works to the advantage of countries with a highly skilled workforce.

Innovation can be a force for both the creation and destruction of employment. Rapid technological change can cause structural unemployment, forcing governments to invest in retraining and the provision of new skills.

Interest Rates

The interest rate is the current price of borrowed money. Like any other price, it is determined by the forces of supply and demand. The demand for money is made up of those holding money prior to spending it, people saving some, and those who are holding it in preference to financial securities. Although government has limited control over the demand for money it can alter interest rates to encourage greater or lower money holding. At present the base rate is controlled by the monetary policy committee of the Bank of England. Once it is chosen, the total money supply must be matched with the demand. This is done through open market operations to buy or sell government securities. The Bank of England will always buy securities from the banks but the price at which it does this is based on the target interest rate. The lower the price offered for the securities, the higher is the interest rate. If banks have to pay more for funds from the central bank, they will be forced to increase the rate charged to customers. All interest rates ate linked to this base rate.

Interest rate changes are now the main monetary policy to manage aggregate expenditure. There is a transmission mechanism, where changes in interest rates work themselves through into the flows of consumer and investment spending. It is questionable how sensitive these flows are to a change in interest rates. It is by no means certain that a cut in interest rates will be sufficient to boost consumer spending in order to stave off, or get out of, economic recession. There is a view that expectations are far more important than short-term movements in interest rates in influencing the volume of investment spending. The economic importance of interest rates lies in their power to influence aggregate demand, and as a tool to influence the balance of payments and economic growth.

see also...

Aggregate Demand; Monetarism and Monetary Policy

International Competitiveness

This is essential for open trading economies if they are to increase their rate of economic growth; it is the long run solution to balance of trade problems. Competitive advantage centres on the concept of productivity in domestic firms compared with that of rival countries. Productivity can be measured in terms of the amount produced per hour of employment. If the unit costs of production fall, this will allow firms to lower their prices without sacrificing profit, hence the expansion in output and employment. Productivity data can appear to rise during recessions simply because employment may be falling faster than the level of production. In order to increase competitive advantage there must be a rise in both the productivity of capital and labour over time. Firms can increase their international competitiveness by:

★ rationalizing production to get rid of high cost plants;
★ relocating production to places where labour costs are lower;
★ process innovation;
★ product innovation;
★ using new management techniques and employment practices;
★ incorporating the latest technology into any investment;
★ sourcing components from abroad but assembling the final product at home;
★ seeking out new market opportunities;
★ improving the relationship with their suppliers and customers.

Suggestions of what governments can do to improve international competitiveness include:

★ encourage inward investment from technology specialists;
★ increase research and development expenditure;
★ increase the skills of the labour force via education and training;
★ improve the economic infrastructure; and access to finance
★ encourage competition between domestic firms;
★ operate macroeconomic policies favourable to business expansion.

Investment

Business investment is the addition to the total stock of capital goods plus any physical increase in stocks of raw materials or finished goods awaiting sale. The motive for investment is to increase output and therefore revenue and profit in the future. Most firms will want to minimize their stocks and this may be involuntary investment when sales fall during a recession. The full name of investment is *gross domestic fixed capital formation*. It includes all the money that firms spend on fixed assets. However some of this spending will be to replace worn out capital stock. *Net investment* is found by subtracting the depreciation or replacement spending from the gross figure.

The importance of business investment stems from its role in the aggregate expenditure flow. Investment can also be the most important factor in the process of economic growth and international competitiveness. In this context it is not just the volume of business investment that is important, the quality of new investment is vital and must incorporate the latest technology.

Economic theory suggests that the level of business investment at any time depends on the relationship between the present value of the expected future revenue from the investment and the current cost. Firms will work out the expected yield on investment projects and compare this with the interest rate on borrowed funds, investing up to the point where the marginal cost or the interest rate equals the expected return on the last pound invested. Investment by its nature is a risky business even after investment appraisal techniques have been applied. Anything that alters expectations will cause the demand curve for investment to shift. Expectations may be a far more important influence on the volume of business investment than short-term changes in interest rates. The pace of technological change, the degree of competition in a market, changes in labour costs and government policies can also influence the level of business investment.

Keynesian Economics

John Maynard Keynes (1883–1946) took issue with the classical school of thought, which suggested that an economy would settle in equilibrium where there were no unemployment. This was at odds with the experience of the 1920s and 1930s, when unemployment reached 25% of the workforce. In the *General Theory of Employment, Interest and Money* published in 1936, he argued that employment is determined by the aggregate demand in the economy. If aggregate demand falls short of aggregate supply or the productive potential, then an economy can stay in an equilibrium with high unemployment. He developed this idea into the suggestion that governments could manage the level of economic activity in a capitalist economy, avoiding the twin evils of mass unemployment and rising prices. By manipulating the components of total spending, an economy could be stabilized at a level close to full employment. He focussed on the injection of expenditure into the system and later incorporated the idea of the multiplier effect. Any injection would have a greater than proportional effect on the total level of income and employment. Economic recovery could not be engineered by cutting wage levels as the classical school argued because this would lower effective demand and deepen the depression by lowering overall spending.

From the 1940s onwards, Keynesian economics became the orthodox macroeconomic theory. By the 1970s it was challenged by monetarism as a tool of economic management. Keynes had little to say on the subject of inflation because it was not a problem at the time he was formulating his ideas. He accepted that if the total demand became excessive when there was full employment then the price level would rise. Keynes did not live to see the success of his ideas, which were modified by a generation of Keynesian economists. He showed that it was possible to stimulate the economy and manage it at a level where unemployment was minimized.

Labour Mobility

There is complete freedom of movement of labour anywhere within the member countries of the European Union. However, labour is relatively immobile between geographical areas. This can be an economic problem if it results in an inefficient distribution of labour with shortages in one part of the economy and a surplus of unemployed labour in another. *Geographical immobility* may be explained by strong social ties to an area, or may be the result of ignorance of employment opportunities in different parts of the country. There may be specific financial obstacles to individuals and families moving area. Perhaps the biggest obstacle to regional mobility is the shortage of rented accommodation and the high property prices in the parts of the country that offer the best employment opportunities. The government can increase mobility by a combination of financial incentives or compensation for a higher cost of living within the new area. Previously, regional policy has focussed on attracting work to the workers (rather than workers to the work). Encouraging higher labour mobility can cause economic problems if it results in overcrowding, traffic congestion, rising property prices and environmental damage in the growth regions.

Occupational immobility refers to the difficulty of moving from one type of employment to another. Again there are frictions in the labour market that prevent easy transfer. The obvious one is the lack of appropriate skills and qualifications for particular occupations. Age, sex, and ethnic or cultural background could also be factors working against individuals in their search for alternative employment. Occupational mobility is vital for a dynamic economy and can be increased through education and training for those entering the workforce or retraining for those caught without marketable skills. Rapid technological and structural change increases the need for greater mobility, but it will only occur if economic incentives exist for workers to move.

Macroeconomics

As a subject, economics can be likened to a large jigsaw puzzle. Microeconomic analysis looks at the detail of all the component pieces. Macroeconomics looks at the whole picture and studies the interaction between the component parts. Much of the discussion in macroeconomics concerns aggregates or totals such as income, employment, the rate of growth of output, the general price level and the overall balance of payments with other countries. Macroeconomic policy is about the ways in which government can manipulate the broad monetary flows in the economy in order to achieve its declared economic and social objectives.

There are forces and events affecting the whole economy that cannot be understood simply from the study of individual markets and industries. Macroeconomic events such as recession, and processes such as inflation, provide a context in which business operates and play a part in shaping business decisions. The economy has always behaved in an erratic manner because of what has been labelled the *business cycle*. Part of macroeconomics can therefore be considered to be stabilization policy. At the outset of studying economics it may be a help to realize that any government has only two main weapons of economic management at its disposal, *monetary* or *fiscal policy*.

Part of the difficulty, and also the appeal, of macroeconomics is the disagreement that exists over both the causes of economic problems and the appropriate solutions. Sometimes action to improve one aspect can make other problems worse. If economic objectives conflict, then subjective or value judgements in decisions add a political element to macroeconomics.

There are different schools of thought in macroeconomics, examples being Monetarist, Keynesian and New Classical. The ability to analyze and evaluate their key ideas in an essential skill for economists.

Marginal Analysis

The margin in economics refers to any boundary or frontier around which change takes place. A firm could be described as marginal if it is breaking even and just remaining in business. The whole economy should operate at the margin of the production possibility boundary if it is to make full use of its scarce resources.

Marginal analysis looks at the *effects of small changes in economic variables*. In microeconomic analysis, production is influenced by changes in firms' marginal cost and marginal revenue. For consumers, the marginal utility gives a measure of the satisfaction obtained from the last unit. The marginal rate of substitution is the rate at which they are prepared to swap one product for another. Marginal consumer surplus is the difference between what the consumer would have been prepared to pay for the last unit and the price they were actually charged. For workers, the marginal revenue product represents the money value to the business of the last worker employed and lies behind the demand curve for labour and in theory, the resulting wage.

There is a mathematical relationship between marginal values and total values. When the marginal value from the last unit is positive, the total value will be rising. When the marginal value reaches zero, the total value will have reached its maximum and when it becomes negative it will pull the total value down.

In macroeconomics, marginal analysis is used to describe the tendency to behave in a certain way when there is a small change in income. In investment decisions the marginal efficiency of capital is the return on the last unit of investment.

In general terms, marginal analysis is at the heart of the problem of choice. A rational choice by workers, firms or consumers involves weighing up the additional or marginal cost of an action against the additional or marginal benefit.

Market Demand

A market demand schedule shows what consumers will pay for a particular quantity of a product at a particular time. It is the *sum of individual consumer preferences* and must reflect effective demand. When demand information is presented graphically with price on the vertical axis and quantity on the horizontal axis, a demand curve will slope downwards to the right. This inverse relationship reflects the law of demand, suggesting that the lower the price of any product, the greater the quantity that will be purchased. What differs between products is the consumers' reaction to a price change. A market demand may be divided into clear segments where the buyers have a different sensitivity to price changes. Perhaps the biggest influence on this reaction is the existence of close substitutes for the product: the closer they are, the greater will be the reaction to a price change.

In economic analysis, the demand curve will be influenced by such factors as the price of the product, the price of related products, income and tastes. A change in the product's own price will lead to an extension or contraction along the demand curve, whereas any other change in market conditions will cause the whole demand to shift position. In real world markets, the conditions of demand are rarely static. Consumer tastes can change suddenly. For example, a perceived health risk attached to consumption can reduce the current demand, with a dramatic effect on the current market price. For most products demand will rise over time, but rising living standards will alter the composition of demand.

Firms in an industry compete for a share of the total market demand curve. The best situation for a firm will be when the demand curve for its product is shifting to the right with time, and consumers are becoming less sensitive to price changes.

see also...
Consumer Expenditure; Market Supply

Market Failure and Government Intervention

The free market system is praised for its contribution to economic welfare. However, there are various ways in which markets fail to give acceptable outcomes.

★ Markets cannot supply public goods.
★ There is no automatic mechanism to increase the consumption of merit goods.
★ Production and consumption externalities are not taken into account.
★ Some markets can be manipulated by producers against the interests of consumers.
★ Free markets can increase the inequality of income distribution.
★ The market price rations goods and services but access to a market is limited by income.
★ There is no guarantee that they will lead to a full employment of resources.
★ Consumers can have limited information on which to make rational decisions.
★ Markets are amoral, they will produce anything for which there is an effective demand even if the majority of citizens find the products unacceptable.

All of these aspects of market failure are reasons for government intervention to improve the allocation of resources. The degree and type of government intervention in markets however remains controversial. The major tools of intervention include:

★ direct provision of selected goods and services;
★ legislation to remove or restrict the supply of demerit goods;
★ market incentives such as taxation and subsidies to change the behaviour of market participants;
★ the use of income tax and transfer payments to increase access to markets;
★ direct intervention in the form of price ceilings and floors to get more acceptable prices;
★ watchdog bodies to regulate activities and protect the public interest.

Market Mechanism

A market does not have to have a physical existence, it exists wherever buyers and sellers are in communication to exchange goods or services at a mutually acceptable price. The market mechanism is therefore *where the forces of market demand interact with those of market supply*. Equilibrium in a market is where the price is acceptable to both parties in the exchange, and where the volume bought matches the volume offered for sale. This is a market clearing price and economic theory suggests that markets will naturally move towards this in order to eliminate the market condition of excess supply or excess demand. In dynamic markets, the price will always be moving from one equilibrium to another because of changes in the conditions of demand and supply. When demand and supply are shown on a diagram with price on the vertical and quantity on the horizontal, the demand curve will slope downwards to the right and the supply will slope upwards to the right. Any shift in one curve will lead to a movement along the other. An increase in demand will raise the market price giving a signal to producers to increase their output. An increase in supply will put downward pressure on the price and consumers will react by increasing the amount they buy.

The market mechanism does not always create an acceptable equilibrium price, or a price which reflects true costs. This kind of market failure can be corrected by government intervention. This does not always lead to an efficient outcome. Unfortunately, the market mechanism works even if the product is illegal.

Markets operate efficiently when resources are fully utilized and consumer wants are satisfied at the lowest unit cost. Some government intervention in the market may limit the market power of producers in order to ensure that the main influence over what is produced lies with the consumer.

Market Supply

The supply side of a market is the combined output of all the firms which are attempting to satisfy comsumer demand. The market structure refers to the number of firms and the nature of the competition between them. There are supply situations where some firms have considerable influence over the market price and others where individual firms have relatively little market power.

The market supply curve shows the total amount offered for sale at any given price at a particular time. The law of supply predicts that the higher the price is, the greater the quantity that will be supplied. The response of supply to a price change depends on the ease with which production can be altered. Time plays an important part in this. The short run is defined as a time when at least one of the firms' factors of production is fixed. The long run is when they can be altered. Some firms can alter output almost immediately whereas for others using more capital, the process of adjustment could take months.

A change in the market price will lead to an extention or contraction of supply but a change in any other supply condition will cause the whole supply curve to shift. The biggest influence on supply at any time will be the firm's costs of production. Anything which increases costs will shift supply to the left whereas a fall in costs will increase supply. Production costs can change because of changes in the price of factors of production such as labour, raw materials and the impact of technology on the production process. Government policy in the form of taxes or subsidies can affect supply as can collective action by producers. The entry of new firms into an industry, motivated by the prospect of abnormal profit will increase the total supply whilst business closures would reduce it.

Merit Goods

A merit good is a product that a free market fails to allocate efficiently. There are two important characteristics that define a merit good. The first is that the good is *undervalued by the consumer*, who does not realize how important it is to their own welfare, or the wider benefit to the community, at the time they make the consumption decision. This may be due to a lack of information or even wrong information about the product. It leads to a merit good being underconsumed and therefore underproduced by firms. Another reason for underconsumption could be that the price at which it is supplied lies outside an individual's purchasing range.

The second characteristic of a merit good is that it has *large positive externalities*. The social benefit of consumption will be much higher than the private benefit, e.g. innoculation. Health, education and training can be considered as merit goods because they are a social investment that will raise productivity, and therefore contribute to a higher standard of living.

It therefore makes economic sense to increase the consumption of merit goods. They can be provided at zero price directly by government agencies or through private firms subsidized by the government. The alternative could be to subsidize the consumers. Voucher systems could allow the consumer an element of choice and encourage competition in supply. The danger with intervention in merit goods is that the government could be accused of *paternalism*, making decisions for individuals rather than trusting their judgement. In the case of education, this may be justified because those making the decisions would be parents but the consumers are the children. The view is that no one should be disadvantaged through the decisions of others. Merit goods differ from public goods which must be provided by government.

> ### see also...
> **Public Goods; Demerit Goods**

Microeconomics

Microeconomics investigates the choices that are made under conditions of scarcity, by consumers and firms. The fundamental choices of a production system involve the decision over what to produce, how to produce, and how the resulting output should be distributed. The difficulty in these choices is that the economic resources have alternative uses and the question of allocation of scarce resources involves issues of equity or fairness.

In microeconomics, economists study the operation of firms within particular markets. In order to understand and predict business behaviour they build theoretical models as a simplified starting point. The models are then refined and the assumptions modified in the light of real world experience. The framework of competition is central in microeconomics, and a comprehensive theory of the firms' behaviour and performance has been developed in different market structures.

In the real world there is no perfect outcome in the market mechanism and markets fail to allocate all resources in a way that everyone finds acceptable, e.g. in agricultural markets; the solutions offered to improve them involve value judgements. One of the difficulties for the economist is in predicting human behaviour – this is why economic forecasts are often wrong. The key assumption is that people behave in a rational manner that will lead to an improvement in economic welfare. Behaviour will be the result of incentives and disincentives. In addition, they may try to anticipate future events. Some explanation of behaviour lies outside the subject boundary. For example, what motivates entrepreneurs? What gives a product value in the eyes of consumers? The economy is a complex mechanism to understand and microeconomics is only half the jigsaw. The behaviour of consumers and producers influences the whole economy but is also influenced by macroeconomic events and government policy.

Minimum Wage

The idea behind a statutory minimum wage is to intervene in the labour market in order to protect the lowest paid from exploitation and to guarantee a minimum standard of living for workers. In economic terms it is aimed at correcting a market failure by not allowing the price to fall to its natural equilibrium level. It is an example of a price floor using the same economic logic as the guaranteed prices paid to farmers under the CAP arrangements.

The economic criticism was that its introduction would cause unemployment among the workers it was designed to protect. The logic was that firms would face higher costs, and would therefore have to raise prices, damaging sales and leading to workers being laid off. There is no evidence of a rise in unemployment caused by the policy. This may reflect employers' ability to pay higher wages or be the result of a buoyant and growing economy. The minimum wage did not apply to young workers. The

justification offered was that people in training had lower productivity and should not expect the full adult rate. If the occupations are low skilled, this may not be a valid explanation and the wage differential could be seen as discriminatory. In a small way the minimum wage has slowed the growth in wage inequality. The occupations where the minimum wage will have made most difference are in catering, parts of retailing, care and cleaning. Since women are over represented in these jobs, the minimum wage may have made a small contribution to reducing the wage gap that still exists between males and females.

The minimum wage is not the long run solution to low pay. Education and training will reduce the supply of less skilled labour, pushing wages up. More people will have access to higher paid work because their productivity will be higher, but there will always be some workers at the foot of the pay ladder.

Monetarism and Monetary Policy

Monetarist theory has tried to explain both the cause of and solution to the problem of inflation. The two key ideas are the volume of money in circulation and its price, i.e. interest rates. The classical quantity theory of money predicted that if the money supply increased and both the output of goods and services and the velocity of circulation of money were constant, then inflation would be inevitable. In the 1970s, the well-known monetarist economist Milton Friedman believed that inflation was always and everywhere a monetary phenomenon. The simple solution would be to reduce the volume of money or to raise interest rates. Monetarist theory also suggested that in the long run, any attempt to raise aggregate demand beyond the natural level of unemployment would lead to both higher inflation and rising unemployment. Monetarism became less popular with politicians because of the uncertainty over the mechanism by which it triggered extra inflation. In addition, reducing the money supply or increasing interest rates to control inflation had a high opportunity cost in terms of employment and economic growth. There were also causes of inflation that were independent of the money supply.

Monetary policy now focuses on the lowest level of interest rate that will achieve the inflation rate target. Responsibility for setting the interest rate now lies with the monetary policy committee of the Bank of England. Monetary policy can also be used to influence the exchange rate. A rise in interest rates would reduce the money supply and raise the exchange rate, but this may prove disadvantageous for the economy. If the British economy joins the EMU, the exchange rate will be fixed and a single interest rate will be fixed for all the members. The national government will be left with fiscal measures in its short-term management of the economy. At present, monetary and fiscal policy are used together, and are complementary rather than substitute policies.

Monopolistic Competition

In this type of market structure, competition is between a large number of small, independent, firms. They all produce differentiated products, giving each one a slight amount of market power. There is an opportunity to charge different prices, but each firm will face a relatively price elastic market demand curve as they are close substitutes for each other. There is complete freedom of entry into the market according to this model, which means that abnormal profit will attract new suppliers. The market share of the existing players will therefore fall and the abnormal profit will be competed away. Product differentiation is what distinguishes this structure from perfect competition. It is this slight element of monopoly power that gives rise to the name of monopolistic competition, though the large number of firms means that the model is the closest one to *perfect competition*.

Firms convey information to consumers through persuasive advertizing. *Branding* is an essential idea in monopolistic competition, as is *product innovation* to keep ahead of rivals. Firms can use these weapons to shift their demand curve to the right. This may postpone the long run equilibrium where abnormal profits are reduced to zero by the entry of new firms. If some firms are able to increase demand and reduce the price elasticity by getting brand loyalty, then the market structure will be effectively moving towards that of *oligopoly*. Internal growth via the investment of retained profit, and external growth via takeover and merger activity will also change the market structure, giving the larger firms an opportunity to raise prices. Firms with lower costs might be tempted to cut prices in order to increase market share.

The economic criticism of this market structure stems from the fact that profit maximizing firms will choose an output lower than the most efficient one. The other source of inefficiency lies in the waste involved in competitive advertizing, which can largely cancel itself out.

Monopoly

In theory, a monopoly is a market structure with a *single seller*. In this situation, the firm is also the industry. The practical definition is where one firm or two acting together, has more than 25% of the market. This figure is deliberately set low so that any potential monopoly situations can be investigated. A monopolist is likely to face a relatively price inelastic downward sloping demand curve. There are large barriers to entry in monopoly and therefore no close substitutes. A profit-maximizing monopolist can make abnormal profit in the short run and the long run. The criticisms of monopoly are based on a theoretical comparison with perfect competition. They are accused of being inefficient and of exploiting consumers by charging a higher price and producing at lower output than a perfectly competitive firm. Price discrimination may further boost a monopolist's revenue. The lack of competition gives a monopolist no incentive to lower cost or to improve the product on offer. On the other hand, it is possible to argue a positive case for monopoly. The security of profits may encourage investment in process or product innovation. Monopolists may experience economies of scale, and have lower unit costs than firms in a more competitive structure. *Natural monopoly* is a situation where it would not make economic sense to have competing firms, because it would be inefficient to have expensive fixed capital duplicated. It is difficult to judge the economic performance of monopolists because it depends on how they choose to behave and what steps a government takes to protect the public interest.

Monopolists can be controlled through taxation, price capping or encouragement given to potential new entrants. Takeovers and mergers can be banned where they would create a harmful monopoly situation.

see also...

Profits and Profit Maximization

Multinationals

Transnational or multinational enterprises are firms with the power to control operations in more than one country. A true multinational would be a firm that operates in many countries across the world and where the revenue from overseas operations were greater than that from its original domestic base. Although some companies describe themselves as global, most have a strong loyalty to the original base. There are now huge flows of direct investment in and out of national economies to build new bases or to acquire firms through takeovers and mergers. Another aspect of multinational activity is to create strategic alliances or cooperation across national boundaries.

Multinationals are a very diverse group of firms and it is difficult to generalize about their behaviour. Much of the economic discussion about multinationals has been conducted in the manner of a cost benefit analysis. It is clear that they bring investment, employment and technology into countries. They have also been criticized for exporting profits to the home base, manipulating their accounts to reduce tax liability in particular countries, paying low wages and exerting political influence. Multinationals' profits can sometimes be at the expense of domestic producers, and their search for higher profits can lead to their moving quickly out of one country and into another regardless of the social cost in terms of lost employment. The driving force behind multinationals' growth has been the search for growth markets and the desire to reduce production costs, hence the locational advantages of developing economies. Governments in advanced countries welcome the inward investment from multinationals because of the impact on growth, employment and even the balance of payments.

Multinationals may continue to grow through diversification in manufacturing and the service sector and the proportion of UK output they account for is likely to rise.

Multiplier Effect

The multiplier effect refers to the effect on GDP of an increase in the level of injections into the circular flow of income. For example, if the level of business investment increased, this would create more income for all those working in the capital goods sector. When their expenditure rises it will increase the output of goods and services and raise incomes elsewhere in the economy. The bigger the fraction of their new income people spend, the stronger will be the multiplier effect: the greater the leakages are, the smaller the multiplier effect will be.

In economic terminology it is the size of the *marginal propensity* to consume that is critical. The government must have an accurate estimate of the size of the multiplier when it is thinking of boosting the level of aggregate spending. Any rise in investment will increase equilibrium income. The increase in consumer spending will cause the demand facing firms to rise, causing them to increase capital investment to meet the new demand. This link between the rise in income and the rise in investment is called the accelerator effect. In a boom, the multiplier and accelerator effect can lead to cumulative expansion. When the economy goes into recession, the multiplier effect can magnify the economic downturn.

The multiplier principle also explains how the commercial banks can *create credit* from any initial bank deposits. Banks must keep a fraction of their assets in a liquid form to meet any transactions by their customers. They will want to lend as much money out as possible in order to make profits. Suppose a bank took an initial deposit of £100 and was keeping 10% back in cash. This would give a credit creation multiplier of 10, meaning that the original deposit would support total loans of £1000 and the bank would have created £900 of new credit. The government could limit this process by increasing the bank's reserve asset requirements.

North South Divide and Regional Policy

Regional inequality has increased in recent decades. This is because of the rapid expansion of parts of the south, coinciding with the relative and even absolute economic decline of other regions. The problem is, that whenever there is structural change in the economy, there is no guarantee that new enterprise will take up the resources released in the declining areas. Regional inequality can be measured by differences in employment rates, income, life expectancy, savings, ownership of consumer durable goods, consumption patterns, crime figures and educational achievement.

The picture of economic inequality is more complicated than a simple north south divide. There are parts of southern England with characteristics similar to parts of the north. Equally, there are economic hotspots in some of the poorer northern regions. Regional inequality casts doubt on the economic idea that the standard of living of all groups of people is rising at the same rate.

Regional policy, through planning requirement and government expenditure, exists in order to achieve an efficient use of resources and greater a degree of equity or fairness. The aim is to encourage the geographic mobility of labour, capital and enterprise to the assisted areas. Since 1973, there has also been access to regional aid through the European Regional Development Fund, and successive governments have encouraged direct inward investment by foreign companies.

It has always been difficult to measure the success of particular regional aid measures; to some extent regions are in competition with each other for the scarce funds. Governments are reluctant to take action which might damage the prosperity in the fast growth areas in order to improve the relative position of the poorer areas.

Balanced economic growth across the regions may be difficult to achieve.

Oil Crisis

The term oil crisis has been associated with periods of time when the available supply has not matched the current demand. In 1974 and 1978, the specific cause of the sudden scarcity was the decision of OPEC (Organization of Petroleum Exporting Countries) to reduce supply. They were able to do this because of their control of a high market share. The economic objective can be seen by applying the idea of elasticity of demand. Oil had a *low price elasticity of demand*, so that any reduction in supply would lead to a large rise in price. The lack of available substitutes meant that consumers bought nearly the same volume at the higher price and as a result OPEC's revenue increased. In addition, oil was an *income elastic product* where a rise in the standard of living shifted the demand curve to the right with time, which put further upward pressure on the world market price.

The term *crisis* arose out of the macroeconomic consequences of the huge rise in price when supply was reduced. It injected a big dose of *cost push inflation* into the economy and this contributed to a fall in incomes and employment.

There is a finite supply of oil and a rising demand. The only way in which oil prices may fall is if the market share of OPEC weakens because of new finds in non-OPEC countries. The appearance of substitute fuels for the petrol engine would reduce the demand for oil and increase the price elasticity, leaving the suppliers in a weaker position to raise prices.

The problem of rising oil prices has been made worse by the political decision to tax the product at 75% of the final price. This was justified as an environmental measure to reduce consumption. However, when price elasticity of demand is low, consumers will carry most of the tax burden and the government will get a lot of tax revenue.

see also...

Collusion and Cartels; Cost Push Inflation

Oligopoly

This is competition between a handful of firms who dominate the market in terms of their market share. Economists use models of competition to predict the behaviour of firms with regard to price and output. It is ironic that the model of oligopoly is probably the most realistic and yet there is no single theory that explains oligopolists' behaviour satisfactorily. In oligopoly the firms are interdependent. Decision making is surrounded by uncertainty and risk, because a firm must allow for the reaction of its rivals when making a decision. Game theory tries to analyse the behaviour of oligopolists in terms of risks and payoffs. The success of a price change depends on what the rivals choose to do; it is because of this uncertainty that prices may stay remarkably static in oligopoly. Firms prefer to use non-price competition based on product differentiation and innovation. One theory of oligopoly suggests that profit maximizing is too risky and there is a strong economic incentive for rival firms to collude and cooperate. Firms may adopt a satisficing approach to business behaviour. One of the problems in analysing oligopoly is that prices can end up being similar as a result of intense competition or as a result of collusion between firms. Examples of oligopoly are found in banking, the car industry, the oil industry and in supermarkets.

The difficulty of obtaining growth at the expense of rivals with similar cost structures may explain the tendency towards takeover and merger activity in markets approaching oligopoly. Diversification may be a sensible option, especially if the product is in the mature phase of its life cycle where product innovation becomes more difficult.
The major economic question about oligopolists' behaviour is whether the firms use resources in an efficient way in the public interest. The Competition Commission will be keen to ensure that there is no collusion and will want to promote competition, in the interests of consumers.

Opportunity Cost

When resources are fixed or limited in supply, and there are competing demands on them, the only way the problem can be resolved is through choice. The opportunity cost of any decision is the sacrifice of the next most desired alternative. Choosing one course of action means a lost opportunity for doing something else. Opportunity cost is not the value of all the rejected alternatives. It is the present *full cost of the next highest ranked alternative*.

Consumers are faced with a budget constraint in the form of fixed income. If they decide to increase the consumption of one product, it has to be at the expense of something else. This is also true for the whole economy. The fixed resources only allow certain combinations of goods to be produced. If all the resources are being used, then any change in preferences will have an opportunity cost. This is why the production possibility boundary is also called the *opportunity cost curve*. It is the slope of the boundary that determines the size of the sacrifice. Generally speaking it gets progressively harder to transfer economic resources from one activity to another, hence the idea that choice will involve increasing opportunity cost. The decision will be a value judgement but the concept attempts to give some precision to the cost of a decision.

Opportunity cost is at the heart of government expenditure decisions. All the real resources going into particular programmes, such as higher education, have alternative uses. The concept of opportunity cost is also relevant for the consumers of the service. Students will have sacrificed earnings in order to get benefit from higher education. Society will have lost output and the opportunity to spend on alternatives in order to invest in them. In the context of firms, a normal profit represents the opportunity cost of all the factor inputs, i.e. they are getting what they would earn in their next most profitable use. It measures their transfer earnings.

Perfect Competition

This theoretical market structure lies at one extreme of the spectrum of competition. The closest example to a perfectly competitive industry is probably agriculture. The economist's model of perfect competition has several assumptions.

★ A large number of buyers and sellers with perfect information.
★ A homogeneous product.
★ Each firm is a price taker.
★ There is complete freedom of entry into the industry.
★ Each firm will be a profit maximiser.

In this structure the individual firm has no market power and is so small that any change in its output will have no effect on the market price. There is little scope for a firm to prosper at the expense of its rivals. Firms can make abnormal profit in the short run if their average cost lies below the market price. They can increase revenue by raising output, and each firm can sell whatever it produces at the market price. If they want to maximize profits they will choose the output where marginal cost equals marginal revenue.

Abnormal profit will be temporary because it will attract new entrants into the industry. This will increase market supply and force the price down. Profit margins will get squeezed until the only firms left in the long run will be ones that are breaking even, making a normal profit. If anything such as a rise in production costs or a rise in market demand disturbs this equilibrium, there will be a new short-run equilibrium. Eventually the mechanism works to restore the long-run position.

The attraction of the model is that each firm will be producing efficiently. There is no opportunity for consumer exploitation. It is survival of the economic fittest because high cost firms will be squeezed out. The model is used to act as a benchmark, against which firms' behaviour and performance in real world competitive market structures can be judged.

Phillips Curve

In 1958, Professor A W Phillips published time series data showing an economic relationship that subsequently was known as the Phillips curve. It was a scatter diagram of the rate of expected inflation on the vertical axis and the recorded unemployment for every year from 1861 to 1957 on the horizontal axis. The line of best fit clearly showed an inverse relationship, as the level of unemployment fell below a certain level, the rate of inflation began to accelerate. The explanation was that as the level of expenditure approached the full employment level, shortages would appear in the labour market and wages would be bid up. Firms would react by putting up their prices. The policy implication of the Phillips relationship was that governments could not achieve full employment and low inflation simultaneously. There was a trade-off between these two macroeconomic objectives.

From the mid 1960s, the hypothesis was challenged. Some economists declared the Phillips curve dead, while others argued that the short-term Phillips curve shifted with time. In the 1970s, extra cost push inflation from raw material prices and labour costs created a situation where higher inflation coincided with rising unemployment and a low rate of economic growth – a combination labelled stagflation. In the 1980s and 1990s the Phillips curve shifted downwards and became flatter, suggesting that a much lower trade-off now existed between the two objectives. The new classical school believed that once the economy had reached a natural rate of unemployment, the short-run Phillips curve would be vertical. Any increase in demand would automatically trigger some inflation. Inflation could be avoided by controlling the money supply and taking action to shift the natural rate of unemployment closer to full employment. Supply side measures would stimulate economic growth and reduce the inflation rate whilst increasing the level of employment.

Policy Conflicts

It is not always possible to achieve macroeconomic objectives simultaneously. Action to improve one aspect of economic performance can damage another. This is the dilemma of a trade-off. Raising the level of aggregate expenditure in the economy can cause an element of *demand pull inflation*; also the high marginal propensity to import means that when consumer incomes rise, the balance of trade tends to deteriorate. Equally, a reduction in aggregate spending to control inflation can damage the chance of getting closer to full employment and by damaging business expectations it can reduce investment spending, which is an important determinant of the rate of economic growth.

In the area of taxation and transfer payments there might be a conflict. High marginal tax rates may raise revenue that can be used to reduce the inequality in the distribution of income but at the same time may damage the incentive to enterprise, which affects both growth and employment.

An example of policy conflict can be seen in interest rate changes. Higher interest rates will reduce investment and consumer spending, normally a bad thing. They will also encourage some capital inflow in the balance of payments and moderate the inflation rate, which is a good economic effect. There are also costs and benefits attached to altering the exchange rate of the pound against other currencies.

Policy conflicts partly explain the growth in popularity of supply side policies. These offer the prospect of falling inflation, rising employment, faster economic growth and an improvement in the balance of payments. Are policy conflicts are a thing of the past? Recently, the government was under pressure to lower fuel prices by reducing the indirect tax on the product. This has two implications: either some other taxes must be raised to make up the lost revenue, or the level of government expenditure would have to be cut. There are still trade-offs after all, and economic policy will always involve some value judgements.

Poverty

This is a tricky concept for economists to define as a distinction must be made between absolute poverty and relative poverty. *Absolute poverty* implies a lack of the basic resources required for survival. In a rich economy, the standard of living will be above this, and therefore the idea is that everyone should have an adequate standard of living. The problem is agreeing on the definition of a poverty line. It is generally believed that economic growth combined with some redistribution of income can remove absolute poverty.

In a free market economic mechanism, there will always be inequality of income in the labour market. There will always be part of the population that does not participate at all and their income is determined by political decisions. The result is that the society has an income ladder. The government can influence its length and the distance between its rungs. However, there will always be some groups at the foot of the ladder and they will be in *relative poverty* in comparison with all the groups above them.

Poverty is more complicated than simply being a lack of income. Family circumstances, expenditure choices, health, education and housing can all play a part in deprivation. In Britain, the extent of relative poverty can be judged by looking at the households who have an income below the average earnings. Some researchers take 50% of average earnings as a suitable definition of a poverty line. Others regard the level of income support payments as the government's view of where the line should be drawn. The Council of Europe has suggested a decency threshold of two thirds of a country's average earnings.

The government wants to reduce the degree of income inequality, particularly *child poverty*, by providing economic assistance to low income families. Government intervention aimed at tackling poverty is always controversial, but it is clear that a free market mechanism will contribute to, rather than reduce, relative poverty.

Price Discrimination

This is where a firm charges different prices for the same quality goods and services. It is usually a technique to raise the sales revenue above that obtained from a single price and can occur where there is a lack of close substitutes. One type of price discrimination would be to charge what the traffic will bear, tapping consumer surplus. This is the difference between what individuals would have been prepared to pay and what the single market price asked them to pay. Another form would be to charge different prices on the basis of the volume consumed. The most usual type of price discrimination is to charge different prices to different groups of consumers in a segmented market. It only works to boost revenue when these groups have different price elasticities of demand, so that a higher price can be charged where the price elasticity is lowest. Car producers have been accused of price discrimination by charging higher prices in Britain than for the same cars in mainland Europe. For price discrimination to work, the market segments must be kept separate by ignorance, time, distance or by the type of consumer. The latter can be seen in age concessions in transport and admissions charges.

One of the problems in identifying price discrimination is that it is only true price discrimination when the product is of the same quality. First class and economy travel is not an example of price discrimination, it is *price differentiation*. Price differences based on the costs of production, e.g. peak and off peak rates, are also in this category and may add to efficiency by spreading out demand.

In economics, price discrimination is usually encountered as a monopoly revenue maximizing practice. It can be justified as a fair business practice if consumers are aware that it exists and are prepared to pay the higher price.

Privatization and Deregulation

From the 1980s these measures were seen as part of the supply side approach to improve economic performance. The idea was to replace monopoly with competition, which would be in the public interest. Privatization took the form of selling shares in what had been nationalized industries and selling publically owned land and housing. Another aspect of the privatization was the opening up of the public sector to competitive tenders from private firms. Activities such as cleaning and catering in health and education were contracted out to the lowest bidder. The economic logic was that this would lead to lower costs and the drive for profits would increase efficiency.

The possibility of creating mixed enterprise where there was a state shareholding in private firms was rejected. Until the time when true competition emerged, the public interest was guarded by regulatory bodies that imposed price controls on the new firms. Price capping was seen as a way of forcing firms to lower their costs, in order to create reasonable profit margins.

There will still be a need for regulation if there is takeover and merger activity or evidence of predatory pricing among the competitors.

The term deregulation has been used to describe a process of gradually reducing the rules by which governments intervene in business. It stemmed from the belief that government intervention was a cause of, rather than a solution to, market failure. Deregulation also meant liberalization in the sense of opening up activities to competition by removing legal barriers to entry. This was part of the contestable market objective. Privatization cast doubt on the economic argument for natural monopoly. This was the idea that single monopolists in some activities might have lower production costs than competitive firms. Although privatization has brought greater choice and in some cases lower prices to consumers, there is evidence that competition is not always efficient and that it does not automatically guarantee higher investment or an improvement in the quality of service.

Profits and Profit Maximization

In economic theory, a profit is seen as the difference between a firm's total revenue, and the total cost of making the output. The *revenue* will be determined by the sales price multiplied by the sales volume. The *total cost* includes all the fixed and variable production costs. The most important distinction is between the concept of normal and abnormal profit. A *normal profit* is the minimum economic return that will keep a firm in business. For this reason, it is treated as a cost of production because it reflects the opportunity cost of capital and entrepreneurship. Firms will be hoping for a revenue high enough to make *abnormal or supernormal profit*. This will be the economic reward for taking business risks, and will provide the economic incentive for producers to attempt to satisfy consumer demand.

In a market with little competition, a firm may charge prices which exploit the lack of substitutes. The resulting profit may be considered excessive, but this is a difficult term to define. It can be the use that is made of abnormal profit, rather than the level, that is controversial. There may be a short-term conflict of interest between using the profit to fund new investment or paying it out to shareholders in dividends. It will be in the long-term interest of all the stakeholders if profits are invested in new products or production techniques.

It is assumed that firms will seek to maximize profits. This would mean producing up to the point where the cost of making one more unit is matched by the revenue received from selling it. Competition between firms can lead to abnormal profit being removed, especially where new entrants are attracted into the industry. This forces firms to focus on cost reduction techniques and ways to boost revenue. Profit maximization is not always the major motivating force, but making profits remains the basic long-term reason for firms' competitive behaviour.

Public Goods

Public goods or collective services, are things which the market mechanism cannot provide effectively. The government provides them from tax revenue. Not all the government services can be considered as public goods because of the specific meaning of the term. Public goods are non-excludable. This means that if the product had a price, there would be no way of excluding non-payers from consuming it. The classic example is street lighting. Some people might pay the price but non payers would still get the benefit. This is known as the *free rider problem*. A private firm could not get sufficient revenue and would operate at a loss.

A public good is non-rivalrous, which means that once a service has been provided, extra consumers do not reduce what is available for the rest. This would also be the case in the street light example. Problems can appear in a public good such as a motorway or a national park. Up to the point of capacity, the good is non-rivalrous, but then marginal users cause less space to be available for the others. It is now exhibiting the characteristics of a rivalrous private good. The problem of traffic congestion can be reduced if people are excluded, e.g. by introducing a toll charge.

The usual case for the provision of public goods at zero price is when its consumption has large positive externalities or benefits to the whole society. The problem might be that a zero price encourages maximum consumption. In the case of health, this may lead to queues for treatment. This has led to the suggestion that user charges should be introduced which would take some of the burden off tax revenue. This would be moving away from a public good towards a *private good*, because it is now rivalrous and the direct charge is making it excludable.

see also...

Health Economics

Real and Money Values

One of the signs of economic progress is the change in output and income over the course of a year measured in money terms. The problem is that when the economy has inflation it raises the money value, and disguises the real change that has occurred. Inflation reduces the purchasing power of any money income, and real income is the change that would have occurred at constant prices. The measure of inflation currently used is the retail price index.

Real income is the new money income multiplied by the base year index divided by the new price index. If they were the same, then money income would be the same thing as real income. Suppose an economy had a GDP of £100 million in year 1 and £200 million in year 2. This would suggest a 100% gain in economic welfare. If there was an inflation rate of 25% between the two years then the real income in year 2 is only £160 million. So the increase in income in real terms between the two years is 60%, even though money income has doubled.

The concept of a real increase is important in discussions on government expenditure. Increased spending on key welfare services is only a real increase when the expenditure has risen faster than the general price level.

Another occurrence is in wage negotiations. Whenever there is anticipated inflation, workers may press for a wage rise greater than the present inflation rate. However the act of asking for an increase can actually cause further inflation, which reduces their real income.

In the discussion of household income, some groups are slipping behind in real terms because the government does not uprate benefits in line with inflation. Pensioners argue that the rise should be consistently higher than the inflation rate and linked to changes in the average wage to stop them slipping further down the income ladder.

Savings

In general, savings are simply any income that is not passed on as expenditure. Consumers, firms and government can all have savings, the most important flow is that from households. These savings form the fund which ultimately finances investment, and therefore it is an important contributor to economic growth. Changes in consumers' decisions regarding spending and saving are important for the current economic performance. Savings represent a leakage of money from the circular flow of income. If savings rise, and if this is not balanced by a fall in the other leakages or a rise in injections into the economy, then it could trigger an economic recession. Savings are the mirror image of consumer spending: the same factors that cause spending to change will also affect saving.

As income rises, economists need to predict what consumers will do with any extra income they receive. This is called the *marginal propensity to consume* and *save* (MPC and MPS). The size of the MPC determines the size of the investment multiplier in the economy. The higher the MPC the greater the effect any increase in the injections into the circular flow will have on aggregate income. Spending or saving is also influenced by expectations of future income and prices. A fall in consumer confidence can lead to higher savings. Savings can be sensitive to changes in the interest rate, but reactions are difficult to predict. Changes in income tax and benefits will alter consumer expenditure and therefore affect the amount saved. If personal wealth increases in value, it can trigger a boom in spending, as can greater availability of credit.

There is now considerable discussion as to whether the low ratio of saving to disposable income is good or bad for the economy. A low saving's ratio implies high current spending which is good for income and employment. A high saving's ratio, with the funds recycled into investment, is vital for economic growth.

Scarcity

In a world of limitless resources, all goods would be free. The basic economic problem for all societies is that resources are scarce. Economics studies the production and allocation of valuable goods and services. Scarcity can be defined as any situation where the demand for resources exceeds the available supply. The *price mechanism* works to ration the use of scarce resources. If the market price rises to an unacceptable level, the appropriate action would be to try to increase the supply and also reduce the demand. Even when it is possible to increase the supply over time, the problem of scarcity will still remain if the demand grows at a faster pace than the supply.

The key idea is that in any situation of scarcity, choices must be made. In the case of the individual consumer, the scarce resource is income and there are unlimited wants. The consumer must prioritize these wants. A similar situation is faced in government spending when tax revenue is fixed.

When there are fixed resources, it is vital to use these as efficiently as possible. Firms will attempt to increase the productivity of scarce factors such as labour and capital, in order to reduce the unit costs of production. In the public sector, competing demands for expenditure have led to a search for alternative ways of raising the revenue to pay for more services. Reorganizing the services to reduce provision costs is another solution. However much the spending on the NHS rises, the level of demand is likely to rise faster; this creates excess demand and queues for treatment.

The problem of scarcity is graphically illustrated in development and environmental economics, e.g. food and water shortages, and the destruction of the scarce tropical rainforest.

In individual markets, a shortage occurs whenever the price is below the equilibrium one. If the market price is not allowed to rise, the only way of allocation will be through physical rationing.

Stakeholding Economy

The basic idea of a stakeholder economy is that the state should intervene in the market mechanism to remove the unacceptable outcomes and achieve economic and social objectives. The view is that *economic opportunity* should be spread widely so that no group is marginalized or excluded from the benefits of an affluent society. One of the most important interventions is therefore in the labour market. Examples of intervention include the minimum wage and measures to reduce discrimination. It is an attempt to apply the idea that everyone has both rights and responsibilities. For example, it is the government's responsibility to protect those who are unable to work via means tested benefits. People who find it difficult to get into work must be encouraged and given skills training but it is their responsibility to try to support their dependants from earnings rather than benefits.

In the context of business, the stakeholding idea has been used to mean that any groups who are affected by business decisions should have an input into the decision-making process. The interest groups might include investors, employees, customers, former employees and local residents. Employee share ownership is an attempt to give workers a bigger stake in the companies they work for. The economic argument is that it will improve labour relations and workers' motivation and productivity. Openness and consultation should be basic features of management. Investment decisions should take into account the effect on the stakeholders and not be geared to the short-term benefits of the firm's shareholders.

Supporters of the stakeholding approach argue that an economy managed by these principles will achieve greater wealth creation. In a stakeholding economy, the government will influence the distribution of income and wealth in an attempt to reduce poverty. The objective is said to be social justice where everyone has a stake in economic success and equality of opportunity.

Standard of Living

The idea of economic well-being is not easily defined. Economists use data on the GDP to measure changes in the volume and value of goods and services produced in the course of a year. It does not take into account any harmful aspects of production, or measure changes in the quality of what is produced. It cannot measure the quality of life that individuals enjoy. There is an assumption that economic growth raises the level of consumption and production, and that higher levels of output reflect a higher standard of living. The problem is that there are a large number of non-measurable influences on economic welfare. Examples include:

★ an individuals state of health and housing conditions;
★ political freedom;
★ the state of the environment;
★ working conditions;
★ the amount of leisure time;
★ the effect of crime;
★ any discrimination that exists.

Indicators of a rise in the overall standard of living hide the fact that not all groups are progressing at the same rate.

For most adults, the most important influence on their standard of living is income from work. There is a big gap between this group and the non-working population, and there are still measurable regional differences in living standards. The government reduces these differences through the provision of welfare services and transfer payments. Higher expenditure on defence or law and order may not always add to welfare, but stops it deteriorating. Economic progress can have costs and benefits via social and lifestyle changes. Some argue that there are medical disorders such as obesity and heart problems linked directly to increased affluence. On balance, each generation is better off – in terms of consumer goods and leisure – than the one before. The decision to increase future living standards by devoting extra resources to investment will be at the expense of the current standard of living of the present generations.

Stocks and Shares

These are financial assets that are bought and sold on the stock exchange and offer the holder the prospect of an income or a capital gain. Stocks are fixed interest securities issued by the government, local authorities or firms. Shares or equities give a variable return in the form of a dividend which reflects the current performance of the business. Shareholders are the owners, and each share is a financial claim on the profits. Unless it is a new issue of share capital, the people buying shares are not contributing to the business capital. There is simply a transfer of ownership of financial capital. The price at which shares change hands does not always reflect the true value of the business assets.

Financial investments involve a degree of risk. There is a direct link between risk and economic return. People will only be persuaded to take higher risk if the expected yield is higher than that of safe alternatives, such as bank accounts. Investors talk of balanced portfolios, which are an attempt to spread risk. The idea is to have a blend of high risk, high yield assets and safe ones such as bonds or gilt edged securities issued by the Bank of England as part of the national debt. Interest rate changes play a big part in the price of these securities. As interest rates rise, bond prices fall and this creates opportunities for speculators to make a capital gain by correctly predicting changes and buying and selling at the right time.

Share prices fluctuate because of changes in company performance and expectations of future events, such as the general economic climate and takeover and merger activity, which will affect profits. Institutional shareholders such as pension funds, insurance companies, investment trusts and unit trusts are responsible for most of the trade in shares, and are more interested in the dividend flows than short-term fluctuations in share prices.

Supply Side Policies

The term refers to any measures that will cause an increase in the aggregate supply or productive capacity of the economy. Policies to influence aggregate supply have always accompanied demand side measures aimed at boosting aggregate expenditure. What has changed is the emphasis now given to the supply side. The objective of supply side policies is to generate a faster rate of economic growth, and to make domestic production more competitive in world markets. This approach will therefore lead ultimately to higher employment and an improvement in the balance of trade. In addition, if market supply increases, prices will tend to fall, so supply side policies will help to control the rate of inflation.

At a microeconomic level, supply side measures could include anything to increase labour productivity or reduce firms' unit cost. Measures might include expenditure on education and training, business investment, and technology. It is the quality and quantity of the factors of production that is the key to economic progress. In the 1980s it was believed that tax reductions were necessary to increase effort, savings and enterprise. The privatization of state-owned assets was also thought to improve the supply side. The deregulation of markets, measures to promote competition, and a reduction in government intervention were seen by the new classical school of thought as essential supply side reforms. The belief was that flexible labour markets were efficient; imperfections on the supply side, such as the influence of trade unions, were damaging growth. Wage push inflation and the loss of output through industrial action were reduced by legislation. The growth of part-time and temporary contracts may have helped to reduce business costs, but have also contributed to greater job insecurity. The supply side policies in operation at the present time seem to be accepted by all the main political parties. Demand management appears to be old fashioned, irrelevant, or even dangerous economics to some observers.

Sustainable Development

One of the central objectives of any economy is to achieve economic growth and a rise in living standards. This is the concept of economic development. The idea of sustainable development is to meet the needs of the present, without compromising the ability of future generations to meet their needs.

Rising demand and increasing expectations are putting pressure on the supply of both non-renewable and renewable natural resources. The aim of sustainable development is to pass on at least the same stock of natural assets so that they can generate a high flow of income in the future. For this to happen, the rate at which finite resources are being used must be slowed down, and the current use of renewable resources must be less than the rate at which they renew themselves. Sustainable growth requires policies of conservation, the recycling of materials, and the use of substitutes for the scarcest resources. Optimists suggest that investment in new technologies will improve the efficiency with which we use resources. When resources do become scarcer, their prices rise, and this provides the economic incentive for both conservation and the development of substitutes.

The concept of sustainability also implies that we should take a close look at how resources are allocated between different countries. The world distribution of income and wealth is highly uneven. Those countries most desperate to get economic growth may take a short-term view about the exploitation of resources. The rich countries use most resources, and can afford to slow the rate of consumption. Sustainable development does raise difficult issues about limiting our demands and the degree of inequality that is acceptable. Value judgements need to be made about what is the best way to protect the world environment and guarantee that everyone shares in the benefits of economic growth. Issues such as global warming and the loss of biodiversity might be an opportunity cost of rapid economic development.

Third World Debt

Some countries have borrowed huge sums of money, in an attempt to finance the process of economic growth. Some of the lending came from surpluses of OPEC countries that were recycled in the form of loans to countries considered to have the potential for growth. In addition, money has been lent by governments as part of foreign aid packages. The economic idea behind the lending is that it will act as a trigger mechanism in stimulating economic growth. There are also loans from the International Monetary Fund (IMF) and the World Bank which help countries that are experiencing severe balance of payments problems. Third world debt has risen because of economic recession, rising interest rates and falling export prices in primary products. Poor countries are under pressure to increase social spending from events such as rising birth rates, falling death rates, epidemics, disasters and inflows of refugees.

Borrowing does increase a country's resources, but the true cost of the debt is adding to the economic difficulties of the poorest borrowers. The IMF and the World Bank impose strict conditions on the borrowers, to ensure that they become more competitive in world markets. Borrowers must agree to cut government spending or raise taxes, devalue the currency, privatize state-owned assets and reduce subsidies and price controls. These measures have a huge deflationary effect in the short term, and cause increased hardship for the poorest people.

Cuts in spending on health and education to pay interest on foreign debt can only harm the prospects for growth and development. Governments in some of the rich economies are beginning to cancel some of the unpayable debt in an attempt to remove this economic obstacle. To stimulate economic growth, loans must be used in ways that maximize the income received by local communities. As incomes rise so will savings and this can fund higher investment and social expenditure.

Trade Unions

These are associations of wage earners aiming to maintain or improve the conditions of employment. The associations act as the agent of the employees in collective bargaining with employers. In economic terms labour is a derived demand. It is not wanted for its own sake but for what it can produce, and the balance of power will always lie with the employers. The central belief of trade unions is that collective action will increase their bargaining power over wage levels and the conditions of work. In the past some unions achieved an element of monopoly power where a high percentage of the workforce were union members. The chief bargaining tool of the unions has always been the threat to withdraw the supply of labour or to impose costs on employers in the event of a dispute. Trade unions may negotiate with management over such issues as wages, working hours and holidays, productivity and manning levels, recruitment, redundancy arrangements and redeployment. They can also act as political pressure groups with wider objectives such as full employment, a fairer distribution of income and better social services.

Trade unions are in a phase of rapid change. Economic events leading to membership decline have altered their bargaining power. One of the recent trends in trade unionism has been the merging of unions into large organisations covering a wider range of occupations. Industrial relations have changed with employers negotiating with single unions for no strike deals, different methods of payment and greater flexibility over working times and work practices. Managements have shown more interest in employee involvement. One of the major changes has been the decline of national pay agreements and the growth of workplace bargaining. The objectives of unions negotiating in this context can differ. Job security and the conditions of work may be more important than pay rises, especially if the firms' profits are not high.

Transfer Payments and Income Redistribution

Transfer payments is the economic term for the social security benefits paid by the government to the non-working section of the population. They are financed through the national insurance and income tax contributions of those people within the production system. An individual's gross income is original income from economic activity plus transfer payments. Income tax and national insurance contributions are removed from this, leaving people with a disposable income. The government can alter the distribution of income by altering original income through policies such as the minimum wage. It can alter the quantity of transfer payments and the amount of money removed in taxation from an individual's gross income. It is, however, the amount of money spent on transfer payments and where it is targetted that will have the biggest impact on the distribution of income.

Governments may attempt to alter the income gap between people. Economists can measure the degree of inequality in the distribution of income and suggest explanations for it. When it comes to measures to reduce it, their role is confined to exploring the costs and benefits of alternative methods.

Transfer payments have grown rapidly and represent the biggest part of a government's welfare spending. One suggested welfare reform is to focus on a means tested approach to transfer payments. Governments must also decide whether the transfer payments will be increased in line with inflation, or as the pensioners want, in line with changes in average earnings in the economy. Another way of reducing the total transfer payments is to try and and get individuals off benefits and into work, though this will not reduce the expenditure on pensions. In economic terms, the maximum amount of redistribution would occur if state benefits for non-workers were increased, and if this were financed by a progressive tax system that took an increasing percentage in tax as the level of original income increased.

Transition Economies

This term is used to describe more than 25 economies in central and eastern Europe that are moving toward a free market economic system following the collapse of centrally planned systems. Most have the characteristics of developing economies. This, together with the difficulties of transition, means that the process of achieving economic stability and growth will be longer than most of the countries' inhabitants hoped. Their key political choice involves the kind of mixed *economy* they want to create. Some are close to joining the EU, but for others the convergence of their economic performance will not be close enough to realize this ambition in the short term.

All of them have faced macroeconomic problems such as rapid inflation, unemployment and huge budget deficits. The attempts to deal with these have caused a fall in output and industrial investment. Falling tax revenues combined with social pressures to increase government spending have made it difficult to reduce budget deficits. The deficits were financed by a combination of borrowing from abroad and increasing the money supply, which added to inflation. Most of the transition economies have also experienced widening trade deficits over time. Perhaps the key to long-term economic progress is to generate a flow of domestic savings that will support investment. Direct foreign investment has been curtailed by the perceived risk of investing in emerging economies.

Creating a market system based on private property rights has involved a massive shift of resources from state ownership to the private sector. This privatization has encouraged enterprise and boosted labour productivity. The downside of free markets is that income inequality has increased, and the inflation has reduced the real income of large sections of the population.

China is in transition from a command economy to a mixed one, and has experienced rapid economic growth.

Transport Economics

Transport economics focuses on the problems surrounding the movement of goods and people within the economy. It is important that future trends in demand are accurately forecasted, so that resources can be allocated to ensure an efficient transport system. Transport investment appraisal uses the techniques of cost benefit analysis; the different policy options however are controversial. Traffic congestion, particularly around city centres, is an example of scarcity. This is predicted to get worse with increasing car use and an increase in the volume of freight transported by road. Road space is only scarce in particular locations at particular times because the demand is highly peaked and this coincides with a fixed supply. Supply side solutions will be very expensive and may have high social cost, and any improvements may simply encourage more car use. Road users do not always pay the true cost of their choice and this encourages greater use and leads to a misallocation of resources, requiring government intervention.

Traffic congestion can be reduced by policies aimed at deterring car use and promoting the use of substitutes by a combination of price measures such as taxes and subsidies and physical rationing. The demand for car use is price inelastic as car owners do not recognise the existence of close substitutes. Transport infrastructure, such as road and rail networks and airports, is largely the responsibility of the government, whereas the provision of transport services is in the private sector.

At the heart of transport economics is the need for resources to be allocated between competing modes of transport. The government is searching for a way of integrating these alternative modes within a coherent structure that meets the needs and reflects the preferences of the users. The government also has a responsibility for regulating transport services, to ensure fair competition, public safety, and that damage to the environment is minimized.

Urban Policy

At the heart of the urban problem is the trend for employment to shift away from the city centres. In the case of manufacturing, the cause is partly in rising rent levels and a shortage of space for expansion. Other locations offer advantages to firms, and lifestyle advantages for employees. At the same time, what employment there is in cities, is mainly in the service sector and is usually taken by people commuting to work from the suburbs. The result is that some areas are left with high unemployment and few job opportunities for residents. This is accompanied by a decaying social infrastructure.

The objective of urban policy is to reverse this trend by focussing on capital investment to regenerate city centres. This must be accompanied by measures to create employment, provide skills training, improve access to better quality housing and to reduce crime. The urban problem requires governments to look at the factors which cause and reinforce poverty in particular areas.

Some regeneration schemes have been criticized because they have not benefited the low income population. A high proportion of new jobs are taken by commuters and where the infrastructure has improved, the resulting rise in property values has pushed rents and house prices beyond their reach. Urban policy has so far failed to attract manufacturing employment on a sufficient scale.

Urban policy may be more successful in the future if there is reluctance to give planning permission for more greenfield site development. This increases the attraction of derelict factory or brownfield sites. There is a theory that the inner city problem is just a mini regional problem, and once new enterprise is attracted in, there will be a magnet effect and the whole area will see cumulative growth. Urban policy will only be successful if the inward investment is permanent and the local population is able to take a full share of the new opportunities.

Wage Differentials

Wages are the price of labour, determined by the interaction of the demand for labour with the available supply. There are many labour markets, each with its own conditions of demand and supply. Economic theory suggests that workers will be in the strongest bargaining position when their labour is vital to the production process, giving a low price elasticity of demand. It also depends on how easy it is for the employers to get access to additional workers. Skilled workers are in the strongest position to press for a pay rise because they are essential, and there are no close substitutes in the short run. Both supply and demand will be relatively price inelastic. On the other hand, unskilled workers may find that they can be easily substituted by machines, and there is a large number of workers available to take their place. The conditions of demand and supply explain why there will be a wage differential between the two groups. Some of the pay gap is traditional, in that certain occupations have always been paid more than others. The gap may be widening, because the demand for less skilled work is falling, while in some occupations there is a skills shortage, and the demand for labour is rising.

In spite of equal pay legislation, there is still a gap between male and female rates of pay in some occupations, with no economic justification. Wage differentials exist between different age groups, it is assumed that experience adds to workers' productivity, and this should be reflected in pay.

The existence of wage differentials raises the issue of the relative worth of different occupations. This involves value judgements because it is difficult to give exact money values to tasks.

Wage differentials persist in the labour market because of imperfections in the form of barriers to the mobility of labour. It is occupational immobility which prevents workers moving into the higher paid jobs.

Welfare State

The problem in defining the Welfare State is that its boundaries are somewhat blurred. The idea behind a Welfare State, is to provide a package of social protection and a range of services as a matter of right to the population. The Beveridge report published in 1942 suggested that the state was responsible for the welfare of individuals from the cradle to the grave. Such a statement would not receive the level of political support now as it did then. The Welfare State was created in different circumstances from the present time. One of the features of discussion on the Welfare State is the criticism of it by people with different political perspectives.

The idea of social protection was to create a safety net, so that people could not fall into poverty because of unemployment, sickness or old age. In addition to transfer payments, the Welfare State is made up of government expenditure on education, health, housing and personal social services. Using this wide definition, the total resources going into the Welfare State represent about 70% of government expenditure each year. The objective is clearly to redistribute resources in favour of those, who for no fault of their own, fall on hard times.

Social change and rising expectations partly explain the growth in welfare expenditure. The economic problem is that the demand is rising faster than supply. There is always a choice in expenditure and the way it is financed.

There is a view that increasing welfare spending by government is no longer sufficient, and there is scope for greater private provision. This means private firms supplying services within education and health, and individuals being encouraged to fund more of their welfare from savings. This would release more resources to be targeted on those in greatest need. The Welfare State may be redefined in future, the economic question is whether the services will be more efficient, and reach their declared objectives.

Other related titles

 TEACH YOURSELF

INFORMATION TECHNOLOGY

Stephen Gorard, Neil Selwyn

Teach Yourself 101 Key Ideas is a new series designed to provide a quick way into a particular subject. Each book contains short accounts of 101 key ideas arranged in alphabetical order. Each account gives an interesting and informative summary of the term, which will be useful whether you are at college or university, or reading for general interest. You need not read the books cover to cover; just dip in when you come across a term you don't know.

Information technology is redefining the world in which we live. Organizations spend billions on it. Data about us is stored on it and communicated across cyberspace by it. Employers bemoan a general lack of skill in using it. But what is information technology, how does it work, where did it come from, why is it relevant to all of us and how can we understand the effects it is having on our lives and on wider society? This book unravels the answers to all these questions helping you gain a clear understanding of the key concepts, people, theories and arguments.

TEACH YOURSELF

BUSINESS STUDIES

Neil Denby

Teach Yourself 101 Key Ideas is a new series designed to provide a quick way into a particular subject. Each book contains short accounts of 101 key ideas arranged in alphabetical order. Each account gives an interesting and informative summary of the term, which will be useful whether you are at college or university, or reading for general interest. You need not read the books cover to cover; just dip in when you come across a term you don't know.

Business touches us all. We are all affected by the business of business – producing the goods and services that consumers want, and making them available at a convenient time and place and at a price the consumer is willing to pay. Most of us, however, have little or no knowledge about the mysteries of business. Its terms, concepts, ideas and theories are often shrouded in obscure language. This book explains and clarifies terms and concepts, outlines ideas and visits some of the theorists behind the theories.

HAVERING COLLEGE OF F & H E

28395